Style in Piano Playing

Peter Cooper

JOHN CALDER
LONDON

First published in Great Britain in 1975
by John Calder (Publishers) Ltd.
18 Brewer Street, London W1R 4AS

©Peter Cooper 1975

ISBN 07145 3512 5

Photosetting by
Thomson Press (India) Limited, New Delhi.
Printed in Great Britain by Unwin Brothers
Limited, The Gresham Press, Old Woking,
Surrey, England.

CONTENTS

ILLUSTRATIONS

To Dorothy L'Estrange Malone,
in gratitude and affection

PREFACE

On my travels as a concert pianist I am often asked what I consider the most important element in piano-playing. My first reaction is, 'the music itself'. In such a many-sided activity, it is well-nigh impossible to select one particular attribute as taking precedence over all others, for it is the combined excellence of many factors which gives pleasure in piano-playing.

If I were forced to give a considered answer however, I would say 'style', with its sub-divisions: the composer's style, the style of his country, the style of the times in which he lived, of the piece itself, of the instrument for which it was written. Then there is the performer's personal style of playing, and how successfully it is adjusted to these others.

In this book I have tried to relate style to the grand piano as it is at present constituted. What I have said about the contemporary pianoforte and its ancestors is based on my experience as a pianist, harpsichordist and piano teacher for forty years. What is not supported by historical fact can only be supplemented by my own judgment.

I leave it to the reader to reject or accept these observations as he wishes.

Part I

CHAPTER 1

EVOLUTION OF THE MODERN PIANO

If Bartolomeo Cristofori, to whom the invention of the pianoforte in 1709 in Florence is usually credited, were able to see today's concert grand piano, he might well be amazed, but the inventors of the first car or aeroplane might be similarly astounded at a racing car or a supersonic aircraft. Whereas the car-driver or the pilot is solely concerned with the present scene, a pianist, operating his high-powered 1970s model, plays works written for the piano over a period of 200 years. He not only thinks and plays in terms of the current instrument, but of the many different kinds of pianos for which composers have written since the pianoforte's first appearance.

Moreover, the pianist does not hesitate to appropriate music written for the more fragile clavichord and harpsichord, the pianoforte's forerunners as keyboard stringed instruments. Nor does he shrink from playing elaborate piano transcriptions from sources other than the keyboard—vocal, orchestral or operatic. In fact, the modern concert grand piano is a kind of musical boa-constrictor, an iron-framed monster which will support a tension of 200 pounds to a string, an overall stress of 20 tons, and a weight of 1,120 pounds. This 'triumph of ironmongery', as Bernard Shaw called it, is usually 8 feet 10 inches long and has a compass of $7\frac{1}{4}$ octaves.

Cristofori's pristine pianoforte was much more delicate. Of the two models extant, the earlier one of 1720, now in the

Metropolitan Museum, New York, is 7 feet 9 inches in length, and has a compass of 4½ octaves. Its wooden frame makes the tension of the strings very weak, and it has no stops or pedals of any kind.

Created in the age of the harpsichord it had a good deal in common with it—a slender shape, because its compass was much the same, and a small sound owing to its weak string tension. It was the method of its sound production which made it so markedly different. No inflection of tone by pressure of the finger had been possible on the harpsichord. To remedy this defect the new instrument was called *gravicembalo col piano e forte* (literally harpsichord with soft and loud). Stretched strings which had been set in motion by the plucking of tiny quills, were now struck by small wooden hammers covered with leather, the resulting volume depending on the speed of the key's depression.

Another Cristofori piano, which dates from 1726 and is in the Musikinstrumenten Museum of the Karl Marx University, Leipzig, has a stop operated by hand for *una corda*, a quietening device so that only one of the two strings to a note sounded. In the course of the century other stops were to be introduced, but none had more effect on keyboard writing and playing than the 'forte' or sustaining stop. Without it the pianoforte would have remained a dry-toned instrument. Its mechanism, which raised the dampers from the strings, was operated first by a hand stop, later by knee levers, and finally by a foot pedal.

Mozart in a letter to his father, dated October 17, 1777, from Augsburg, where he had visited the piano-maker Johann Andreas Stein, writes:

'The pedals, pressed by the knees, are also better made by Stein than by anyone else; you scarcely require to touch them to make them act, and as soon as the pressure is removed not the slightest vibration is perceptible.' Knee levers are to be found on the pianoforte made for him by Anton Walter in Vienna (Mozart Museum, Salzburg). These raise the dampers to the right and left of the player in two sections, enabling the treble or bass to be sustained independently.

In the Raymond Russell Collection of Early Keyboard

Pianoforte by Bartolomeo Cristofori 1720. The dimensions are: Length, 7 feet 7 inches; width, 3 feet 3 inches; depth, 9½ inches. There are two strings to each note (the vibrating length of the longest is 6 feet 2 inches; the shortest 4 inches). Its compass is four octaves and a fourth—C to F, and it does not have a pedal.

The Mozart Piano, built by Anton Walter, at the International Stiftung Mozarteum SALZBURG.

Beethoven's piano, made by Konrad Graf in Vienna. Courtesy Beethoven House, Bonn.

Instruments (St. Cecilia's Hall, Edinburgh) there is a piano by the Dutchman Americus Backers (London 1772) with pedals which operate unusually through the shafts of the two front stand legs. The left or soft pedal moves the keyboard to the right for 'una corda'; the right or 'forte' pedal raises the dampers off the strings. In 1783 in London John Broadwood patented his device of a sustaining pedal placed on a lyre with the soft pedal, immediately in front of the player.

In the late eighteenth century, harpsichord, clavichord, and pianoforte (or fortepiano as it was sometimes called in Germany and France) co-existed quite happily. Harpsichord and pianoforte often had interchangeable characteristics, and the early eighteenth century pianoforte could be regarded as a harpsichord with a new kind of action, i.e. hammers. The sustaining pedal was the first of a series of inventions which was to establish it as a separate instrument, a process which continued in the nineteenth century, the period of its great development, and eventually isolated it completely from its older cousin.

Like the harpsichord the early pianoforte acquired a number of stops to give it additional tone-colour, devices which could muffle the sound, imitate lute or harp, even the harpsichord itself. Towards the end of the century these mechanisms were transferred to foot-pedals, with a number of new piquant effects introduced from Turkish music: bassoon, drums or triangle. Mozart's Rondo alla Turca, the concluding movement from his Sonata in A major (K 331) must have been far more gaudily vulgar on a piano 'with Turkish effects' than the polite, refined piece it usually is to-day.

A piano made by Erard in Paris in 1803, which was in the possession of Beethoven, had four pedals—lute, sustaining, mute and una corda (Kunsthistorisches Museum, Vienna). Also in the same museum is one by Conrad Graf (Vienna c. 1820) which had five—bassoon, two mutes (one half strength, the other full) una corda and tre corde (sustaining). Yet another by him in the possession of Brahms, and before that of Robert and Clara Schumann, had four pedals.

In the course of the nineteenth century the 'fancy'

pedals disappeared and only the soft and sustaining pedals survived. (A third or middle pedal is found on Steinway concert grand pianofortes today—a Steinway invention from America in 1874. By means of a rail which pushes up certain notes already struck, higher than the dampers, these notes may be held without participation by the hands, independently of the sustaining pedal).

Cristofori's piano had an escapement for the hammer and the pianoforte later became more efficient in its action through the invention of double-escapement by Sebastien Erard Paris (1821) which made for an easy and quick repetition of the key. Rosamond Harding in her *History of the Pianoforte* (Oxford University Press, 1933) says: 'Without this action the art of pianoforte playing could not have attained the state of perfection to which it has now risen; in fact we may say that modern pianoforte technique was built upon it.'

Ignaz Moscheles noted in his diary after the new invention: 'This quicker action of the hammer seems to me so important that I prophesy a new era in the manufacture of pianofortes.'

Meanwhile with additions to its compass in both treble and bass the pianoforte's sonority was increasing. By the middle of the nineteenth century its keyboard span had reached 7 octaves. To support the additional notes iron entered into its frame from 1800, and in 1851, according to A.J. Hipkins (*History of the Pianoforte,* Novello) Broadwood's iron grand model was the first pianoforte to be made in England with a complete metal frame. He had been preceded by Jonas Chickering in Boston, who in 1843 patented a frame for grand pianos in one solid casting. As with most inventions the iron frame was not specifically the work of one individual, but the result of experiments on upright, square and grand pianos by several people for half a century. Without the iron frame the piano would never have attained the power of which it is capable now.

At about this time felt began to be used instead of leather in the hammer heads, which further thickened the tone; and overstringing (Steinway in America, 1855) increased power still more through a greater length of string.

By 1880, thanks to inventions in Europe and America, the pianoforte had been transformed from Cristofori's pioneer model into a new instrument, bearing little relationship to the harpsichord, which was now relegated to the status of an interesting historical piece. Until the outbreak of the first World War in 1914, a wonderful period of piano construction now occurred, which has never been surpassed. Surviving pianos of all sizes, both grands and uprights, are proof of the high level of craftsmanship of these years. Pianos not only had a rich sound, they also possessed a mellow tonal beauty.

A Bechstein full-sized grand, made in 1898, and taken out to New Zealand by Paderewski for a concert tour in 1903 (now privately owned by Mr. J. Hanna of Tokoroa) testifies to the craftsmanship of its time. In 1968, seventy years after its construction, its original soundboard and action were of such excellence that it took one back nostalgically to a great era of piano-making and piano-playing, when beautiful tone, ease and evenness of touch were held in high regard. Its strings have been renewed and felts replaced by the original makers in Berlin, but it retains an integral richness and a ring in its tone which would be hard to find today. Not only were these vintage years for the piano in Germany, but French pianos also had a similar outstanding quality.

Between the two World Wars, traditions were maintained by the great piano houses of Steinway, Bechstein, Blüthner and Bösendorfer, although the previous 'golden age' seemed to have lost a little of its brightness.

Startling changes were apparent after the second World War. Now the piano, in all its models, from the largest to the smallest, seemed to be 'utility', lacking the charm of its pre-War predecessors. Perhaps it was inevitable after the devastation of a war of much greater dimensions and widespread aerial bombing. The division between East and West Europe, one of the legacies of the war, cut off the supply of those pianos whose manufacturing premises lay behind the Iron Curtain.

The new post-war concert grand seemed to aim at

quantity rather than quality of sound, and heavily weighted keys did not make for an easy touch. Often its tone was lack-lustre and metallic, sometimes strident and harsh. On the latest instruments to come out of the great factories, however, there are signs that ease of action is being improved, but much of the pianoforte's pre-war tonal charm is missing.

From the eighteenth century there have, of course, been smaller pianos, upright, square or grand. It was on a square piano that Johann Christian Bach, J. S. Bach's youngest son, is supposed to have given the first solo performance on the pianoforte in London in 1768. The square piano, sometimes erroneously called a spinet, went out of fashion in the nineteenth century—no bad thing, as it generally looks better than it sounds and is now valuable only as a piece of furniture. It was very popular for about 100 years, but its clavichord-like design and shortness of string gave it a very thin sound.

The upright piano, which dates back to the first half of the eighteenth century, has retained its popularity. Like the smaller sized grands it is more suitable for the home than the concert platform. It reached its maximum size at the end of the nineteenth century, but models are more modest in build now.

Every piano firm seems to have one model which is vastly superior to its others. The maker of a superb 8 foot 10 inches concert grand rarely reaches the same standard in a 6 foot model or an upright; or if his 6 foot model is outstanding, the others will be of lesser interest. It is not difficult to think of excellent upright pianos whose quality is never reached in the same company's grands.

More care seems to have been lavished on the construction of smaller grands and uprights in the early nineteen hundreds than now, judging from the tone of both types.

The contemporary grand piano could hardly be called a graceful or elegant instrument, but it is well suited to the cavalier treatment it often receives from today's composers and pianists. Its chief deficiency is in tone; it has a lack of expressiveness which sometimes makes it an exasperating instrument to play, and it is far from possessing the mellowness of its pre-1939 forerunner.

The second World War had a shattering effect on piano-playing by the interruption to piano-production. In the second half of the century, a new type of piano and, consequently pianist, has emerged. No longer is there respect for quality of touch, because on this new piano it cannot be cultivated. Composers for the contemporary piano are unfortunately no longer composer-pianists as were the great figures of the late eighteenth early nineteenth centuries. They do not write gratefully for the instrument because they cannot play it.

It is a great pity that Benjamin Britten, who is one of the rare composer-pianists, should have written so seldom for the instrument. One wonders what the great pianists of the 1920s would have thought of the contemporary piano and whether they could produce from it the sounds for which they were celebrated. Could de Pachmann have made his ravishing tonal effects on our piano? The pianistic susurrations of Cortot or Gieseking in Debussy and Ravel would be difficult to achieve on today's piano.

Going back further in time, it is hard to find any really 'pianistic' music to which our piano is suited when compared to a pre-second World War instrument. Its metallic tone is fatal to the charm and irridescence of Debussy. There is often a lack of evenness in tone-quality in the notes of a simple melodic line of Chopin or Schumann. It is sometimes said that Beethoven would have preferred the breadth of the contemporary piano, but he could get a far finer pianissimo effect on the piano of his day, and one doubts whether he would have appreciated the present grand piano's booming sound. The contemporary concert grand plays havoc with the texture of Haydn and Mozart sonatas and concertos; its massiveness militates against their crystalline beauty.

The piano can more often suggest than state specifically; it is an all-purpose instrument, which may account for its popularity, but it lives more by illusion than reality. In common with other keyboard stringed-instruments it cannot sustain a note as can the stringed instrument or the organ. The note is dying from the moment when it is sounded. When notes are repeated an exact legato is impossible, although the all-important sustaining pedal can help to give the impression of legato. It can only imitate wind instruments or the human voice, for it lacks their real character.

Its fundamental dependance on the sensitivity of finger pressure rather than stops for its dynamics is its principal advantage and *raison d'être,* and only the clavichord can rival it faintly here. The piano has much more volume than the harpsichord, but it lacks the latter's colour which derives from its several sets of strings. It has not the organ's unsentimental directness of attack, nor again its range of tone-colour.

The piano may combine something of all these instruments: the boom of the organ, sensitivity of the clavichord, brilliance of the harpsichord. But as a hybrid instrument it is not as satisfactory as each in its own way.

CHAPTER 2

CLAVICHORD AND HARPSICHORD

The Clavichord

To create his new pianoforte Cristofori drew on two sources: the harpsichord for its keyboard and case, and the dulcimer, a folk instrument, for its method of sound production. The strings of the dulcimer were struck by hammers held in the hands, as with the present day Czimbalom in Hungary. As the hands were engaged on the keys of the pianoforte Cristofori had to find a hammer mechanism to act for them. His invention is the basis of today's more complicated apparatus.

The most delicate and expressive of the early keyboard instruments, the clavichord, can be traced back to 1404, when it was mentioned in a poem, 'Der minne Segel', but it probably existed before then. Small enough to be placed on a table, it was oblong in shape, and its strings, which were of weak tension ran sideways to the player. They were touched by small metal tangents to produce sounds which were beautiful, if minute. The clavichord's expressive qualities endeared it to several eighteenth century composers. Carl Philip Emmanuel Bach appreciated its sensitivity, Mozart used one for composing, which is now in the Mozart Museum, Salzburg. It was an intimate instrument for the study, never for the concert-hall. Its tone could be inflected slightly by discreet finger pressure, and it was the only keyboard instrument to imitate the vibrato of a stringed instrument. This 'bebung' or tremolo was effected by moving the finger quickly up and down, after the key had been depressed.

During the seventeenth and eighteenth centuries the clavichord's small compass of four octaves gradually increased to five. It was typical of eighteenth century fastidious taste that an instrument which produced such lovely sounds, often had a painting inside the lid to delight the eye.

Like the harpsichord the clavichord retreated before the pianoforte's advance in the nineteenth century. In our time it has achieved a come-back, appreciated as an elegant and tasteful medium through which to interpret music of the eighteenth and earlier centuries. Any forcing of tone on the clavichord affects its pitch, and its delicacy can only do good to a pianist's touch. It is an illuminating guide to the more expressive Preludes and Fugues of J. S. Bach's Well-Tempered Clavier.

The Harpsichord

Much more flamboyantly extrovert, the harpsichord's brilliance and bright tonal quality were the antithesis of the clavichord's quietly expressive nature. Here was no gentle sound to be coaxed from a diminutive instrument. With a length of 6 feet upwards, the strings running backwards from the player, it was capable of a blaze of thrilling sound. Hard quills plucking at strings naturally produced a piercing effect, in contrast to the clavichord's modest tangents pressing against them. It might have three or four sets of strings at its disposal. If it had two keyboards, the upper 8 foot set might be of different timbre from the lower. The 4 foot strings, tuned an octave higher, added sparkle to the tone. The 16 foot, an octave lower, could be used with telling effect on selected bass notes, or in conjunction with the 8 foot, if a dark tone-colour were appropriate. There might be a coupler between the keyboards to give more strength when needed, a lute stop whose strings were plucked near the bridge of the instrument, giving an oboe-like tang to the tone, or a harp stop, which produced a semi-damped pizzicato. All these stops were operated by hand at first, later transferred to pedals. Leather points or plectra replaced the quills.

Unlike our age, which favours specialization, an eighteenth century executant would be familiar with clavichord, harpsichord, the new pianoforte and probably the organ as well. Nowadays a pianist would be regarded askance if he played even the harpsichord, although any acquaintance with it will soon convince him that it is a far more exacting instrument than the piano, requiring a finer and more precise finger technique, apart from the extra activity of registration. The piano may make more noise, but contrary to popular belief, the harpsichord calls for more musicianship and deeper perception. Not only were players more versatile in earlier times but instrument makers were more interprising also. Burkhardt Shudi and John Broadwood, two of the pioneers of piano construction at the end of the eighteenth century, were very proficient harpsichord makers. Sometimes the characteristics of both instruments would be intermingled, as for example when they made a harpsichord for Joseph Haydn in 1775, which could produce a crescendo or diminuendo by means of a shutter or Venetian swell, operated by a pedal (Kunsthistorisches Museum Vienna). Silbermann, Cristofori, Pleyel and Erard were others who made both instruments. Today the division is sharp between the two kinds of manufacture; harpsichord makers are not usually large firms, but individual craftsmen, personally directing their work.

Unlike the pianoforte, which became uniform in design from the middle of the nineteenth century, harpsichords varied greatly from country to country, those of France, Germany, Italy and England having totally different features of construction. Perhaps the various designs had their influence on styles of playing in these countries, and this might partly explain how J. S. Bach could differentiate between them in his keyboard compositions.

These variations in design still exist; German harpsichords are usually the most comfortable for the player, as stops are more equally distributed between hand and foot than with other makers. French harpsichords often disconcert by having an opposite system of pedalling to the usual. English terms for lute and harp stops are interchangeable with those on German harpsichords. Instruments by Dolmetsch,

Goff or Goble, to name only three modern English makers, show greatly varied characteristics of tone, touch and design. Thomas Goff of London fashions an elegant instrument, which combines some of the best features of clavichord and harpsichord in its unique range of tone-colour, a superb ease of action and expressive shading more usually associated with the piano.

Among older harpsichords seventeenth century Italian instruments had a tonal beauty which it would be hard to better today. Their remarkable clarity is recalled in the modern instruments of Kurt Sperrhake in Passau, West Germany. Those who want a copy of a particular type of harpsichord—a model of the time of Couperin or Bach, for example—will have no difficulty in finding makers who specialise in reproducing them, but their limited compass confines performance to the works of their own period. Neupert in Bamberg and Michael Thomas in London are two makers who have very successfully copied older instruments. Pleyel in Paris made a very high-powered instrument to Wanda Landowska's specifications, which proved to be exhilarating in the bigger works of Bach, if a little monotonous in its insistent brilliance. In a sense the modern harpsichordist has a more exciting time than the pianist in that the constructional differences of each instrument have to be explored and used to their best advantage, whereas a piano has the same design anywhere.

In the nineteenth century the harpsichord was eclipsed by the steadily developing pianoforte. Harpsichord recitals did not die out, but they were rare. Ignaz Moscheles played a harpsichord during one of his concerts in London in 1837, and Ernst Pauer played older instruments in recital. In 1889 Pleyel made a harpsichord (Kunsthistorisches Museum, Vienna) based on an instrument by Taskin, possibly the one in the Raymond Russell Collection, Edinburgh. This beautiful harpsichord stimulated a renewal of interest in the instrument which has increased, so that it is now easy to hear music composed for the harpsichord played on a modern harpsichord, rather than on a piano.

It is a pity that Raymond Russell decided to omit the chapter on modern harpsichords in his handsomely produc-

A Neupert pedal harpsichord.

A 2-manual Concert Harpsichord by Thomas Goff made
in 1967, based on a harpsichord by Kirkman (1777).
2 keyboards, 7 pedals and 4 strings to each note-16 foot,
8 foot and 4 foot (all leathered on the lower keyboard),
8 foot leather and lute stop (quilled stop) on the upper
keyboard, coupler and harp stop.

Clavichord with 2 strings to each note by Thomas Goff, the lid painted by Roland Pym ("Actaeon and Diana") made in 1960.

A Steinway piano.

ed *Clavichord and Harpsichord.* (Faber and Faber, 1959) but in his paper 'The Harpsichord since 1800' *(Proceedings of the Royal Musical Association,* Vol. 82 12/3/56) he tabulates the differences between old and new harpsichords, noting the change from quill to hard leather in the plectra. He also points out that very few old harpsichords had a 16 foot stop and that weighted jacks, bushed and weighted keys, were formerly almost unknown. He also mentions the half-strength devices sometimes found in modern instruments.

To criticize present-day makers because they have made alterations in the structure of the harpsichord is hardly fair. We do not expect piano manufacturers to keep to Cristofori's model. Instruments, like music itself, must develop; they are continually changing, due either to shifting conditions of construction or to new materials. We may prefer older harpsichords or pianos, but we can hardly stem innovation or the evolution of fashion.

We can for instance, discreetly use a 16 foot stop on a modern harpsichord, particularly in the clavier music of J. S. Bach, who as an organist would have had this stop at his disposal. To restrict modern players to 4 and 8 foot pitch in eighteenth century harpsichord music makes for dullness of tone-colour. 4 and 16 foot pitch without 8 foot is consistent with baroque organ registration, and is very effective where appropriate, particularly in a light quick movement such as the Prelude to the English Suite in A minor. However, the 16 foot stop on the harpsichord which is supposed to have belonged to J. S. Bach, now in the Stern Conservatorium of Music, Berlin, is assumed to have been a later addition. The 16 foot stop is not so appropriate in the Sonatas of Scarlatti, which become too heavy, if so overloaded.

Occasionally, heavily-weighted keys on a modern harpsi-chord make playing more strenuous than on a contemporary piano. The half-pedals mentioned by Mr. Russell add expression, although they do not make the task of the harpsichordist's feet any smoother. But they do provide two levels of tone, piano and forte, to the 4, 8 and 16 foot stops and can be used stylistically in accordance with Bach's rare dynamic markings in the concerted works. A slight crescendo or diminuendo is possible through these half-pedals, but this need not be regarded as a mortal sin. After all, they were possible on an eighteenth century harpsichord which had a Venetian swell. Are we to deny expressive playing of harpsichord music? It is music, gloriously moving at times, and not merely a digital exercise.

A harpsichord was never intended for a large hall, and it is unsuitable in surroundings which suit a symphony orchestra. Neither was it built for performance with large groups of players, though discreet amplification is acceptable if there is no distortion of tone. Some makers, for example Karl Wittmayer of Western Germany, have added electronic amplification, the volume of which the player can control by a knob.

Virginal and spinet are smaller domestic versions of the harpsichord. The virginal, similar in shape to the clavichord, is particularly apt for Elizabethan music, although the term 'virginalles' in the sixteenth century included the harpsichord. The spinet is wing-shaped, with its strings running diagonally from the player. Like the clavichord, both virginal and spinet are made at the present time.

Twentieth century composers who write for the harpsichord do not usually write in a idiomatic style for the instrument, because of the break in the nineteenth century, when stringed keyboard composition centered round the piano. Blocks of chords in quick succession are foreign to the harpsichord; it cannot support a violently percussive style, and intensive experiment is needed before modern techniques of composition can be applied to it. Ligeti's brilliant Continuum (1968) is a very successful excursion into spiky contemporary sound as applied to the harpsichord. It demands a virtuoso technique and a first-class harpsichord, in view of the trigger-like repetition at the end. A fascinating exploration of tone-colour on the modern harpsichord is made by Hans Werner Henze in his imaginative Lucy Escott Variations (1963), best realised on a mellow instrument of Thomas Goff.

Herbert Murrill (1909–52) cleverly combined eighteenth and twentieth century styles in his colourful Suite à la

Française (1938). Delius's unidiomatic Dance for Harpsichord was merely the transference of a piano piece to a new medium, as a tribute to the harpsichordist Mrs. Violet Gordon Woodhouse.

CHAPTER 3

THE MODERN PIANO AND MUSIC OF THE PAST

No matter how much it owes to the past a keyboard instrument is essentially a product of its time, reflecting the contemporary style of composition and playing. A fortepiano of 1790 was not suitable for harpsichord music by J. S. Bach, written only fifty years before. The same fortepiano would be too prim and starchy for a Chopin Nocturne written fifty years later. In the 1970s it is difficult to realize in full the romance of the Nocturne on the impersonal iron instrument which the concert grand piano has now become. Styles of playing change with the character of the piano, which may be ideal for contemporary composition, but is not so for music of the past.

It is a pity we cannot truly produce an instrument of the period in which a composer wrote, but even if we could, it would only be one of the many kinds available to him, as there is no such thing as the Bach harpsichord, or the Beethoven piano. Inevitably as he reaches back into the keyboard music of the last four hundred years a pianist encounters many stylistic difficulties. In his *Harpsichord Manual* (Bärenreiter Verlag, 1960) Hans Neupert points out the relation between period and instrument:

> Today we know something of that mysterious affinity between the music itself and the technique in the construction of instruments, by which in all periods of

music history the potentialities of the instruments to sound go hand in hand with the goals of musical expression, so that the musical ideal of each period requires its specific medium, peculiar to it alone.

This last phrase pinpoints the crux of the problem. Occasionally an authentic instrument of the composer's time, restored, is available, or a modern version of an earlier harpsichord or piano. This is the closest that it is possible to get to an idiomatic account of an older work, but it remains a compromise in view of the renovation or reconstruction that has occurred. Unfortunately the practical playing life of any stringed keyboard instrument, without restoration, is rarely more than twenty years.

What is the pianist to do? Capitulate entirely to his instrument and play everything as though it had been written for his instrument? Or try to adjust his tone to suggest the original medium? His biggest stylistic hurdle will be the leap from harpsichord to piano about 1770, when there was a break in the life-line of keyboard music. But far from dying it took on a new life-line, stimulated by composers of genius centred in Vienna for the next fifty years and stirred up by romanticism for another fifty years after that. What would the piano repertoire be without Haydn, Mozart and Beethoven, Chopin, Schumann and Liszt? Yet none of them wrote for the instrument which the piano has now become, unsuitable in its heaviness for Haydn and Mozart, destructive in its hardness of tone for Chopin.

Would it be better if a pianist avoided harpsichord music altogether and in his recital programmes kept to piano music, venturing no further back than Clementi, Mozart and Haydn and halving the normal span of available keyboard music? We would lose the early composers for the virginal and harpsichord, whose delicate works are of necessity greatly inflated when performed on the pianoforte, but who left some charming music among a mass of experimental writing. Byrd and Gibbons, Bull and Farnaby and a host of lesser known, often anonymous English composers, belonging to the late sixteenth and early seventeenth centuries, make up a piquant school, whose bizarre titles, false harmonic relations, repeated notes, scale passages and profuse ornamentation colour the beginnings of keyboard music. Some of the twentieth century arrangements are by no means an improvement on the original texts, and it was not helpful of nineteenth century editors to omit the ornamentation, when preparing their work for the piano, for where it seems a little excessive, it can be tactfully reduced or omitted; but at least it should be retained in the published copy as a guide to the player. The utmost delicacy of touch is necessary when playing these pieces on the piano. The 'primitives' of keyboard music, they are refreshing to the ordinary listener as well as interesting to the musician.

One feels more at ease with the harpsichord music of Purcell and his contemporaries, whose music shows a remarkable advance in sophistication on early seventeenth century composition, and we would be distressingly worse off without the keyboard works of J. S. Bach and Handel on the piano, wrong as they sound on it.

Carried away by the improvements in the construction of the piano, and a wonderful school of composition and playing which explored its beauties to the utmost, the nineteenth century regarded all keyboard composers of previous centuries as piano composers. Piano came first, style second. Editions of eighteenth century and earlier music were prepared which imposed nineteenth century tastes on it. This was the century of personal expression. Editor and interpreter imposed their views, consonant with the capabilities of the instrument, on all music.

The 'piano first' treatment of harpsichord music has had its exponents in the twentieth century. It was at its most rewarding in the performance of Vladimir Horowitz of the Scarlatti Sonata in B minor (Longo No. 33) in the 1930s. The line of the music was preserved, which made it acceptable stylistically from an eighteenth century point of view, and he produced the most ravishing sounds from the piano, which made the listener forget all about the harpsichord. It was a hybrid performance, an anachronism, as is all harpsichord music on the piano. But the playing was so deeply felt that the work emerged in its sombre splendour:

In another B minor Sonata of Scarlatti (Longo No. 449) Arturo Benedetti Michelangeli imitated harpsichord timbre on the piano most successfully. His seeming transference of this work to an eighteenth century harpsichord was a triumph of stylistic pianism:

There was no dryness in the playing of either sonata, both pianists using the sustaining pedal discreetly and sensibly. Those who forbid the use of the sustaining pedal when playing harpsichord music on the piano ignore, or are ignorant of, the naturally bright tone of the harpsichord. Each jack has a small thin strip of felt to dampen the sound, but this does not work so throughly as the piano's thicker damper mechanism. Consequently there is a slight lingering of sound after a string has been plucked, giving the harpsichord a natural sustaining quality of its own. Absence of pedal, when appropriate, in pre-piano music, only makes a dry-toned instrument drier.

A third 'no nonsense' approach to Scarlatti on a modern piano by the German pianist, Karl Engel, leaves a stern Northern impression on a sunny Mediterranean composer. In a realistic approach which neither attempts pianistic beauty nor harpsichord charm, the result is straightforward, rather faceless music which makes us conscious of the leaden tone of a contemporary piano.

Sonata in D. major, Scarlatti, (Longo No. 461) :

A non-legato or finger staccato touch is appropriate to quick semi-quaver movement in recalling crisp harpsichord sound on the piano. When the switch from harpsichord to piano was made, it was as though the engraver's sharp point had been exchanged for the painter's soft brush. A detached touch on the piano helps to counteract the softening of tone. In aiming at the harpsichord's translucence, it is better if a pianist concentrates on finger, wrist and forearm, rather than the whole arm.

One of the difficulties in transferring harpsichord music

to piano is that the music is often emasculated in the process. The pianist tends to 'soften up' a score in order to lighten his tone, whereas the harpsichord has a natural trenchancy of attack even in the lightest of textures.

Clavichord music on the iron grand is even more difficult to essay. J. S. Bach did not stipulate which instrument, clavichord or harpsichord, he had in mind when composing the Well-Tempered Clavier. Some Preludes and Fugues seem naturally more suited to one than the other, the more fragile suggesting the clavichord, the more brilliant the harpsichord. In any case none is at ease on the grand piano, nor in a large hall, where they have to be blown up well beyond their natural size. Sviatoslav Richter solved this problem very successfully in London's Festival Hall some years ago when he played a number from Book I. He calculated the volume of sound which would suit the Hall's acoustics to a very nice degree, with the result that they emerged with a satisfactory texture on an instrument, and in surroundings quite foreign to their nature. It was matter-of-fact playing that took a twentieth century pianoforte view of them.

When playing early piano music the pianist lightens his tone to suit the shallow touch of the fortepiano and the light action of the early nineteenth century wooden-framed pianoforte. Any trial of Mozart's restored fortepiano in the Mozart Museum, Salzburg will convince the player that we shall never hear his keyboard music (or that of his contemporaries) as he heard it on such a delicate sweet-sounding instrument. On the heavy-actioned modern grand the touch can be lightened by playing 'on the nails', or with flat fingers.

On the piano, tone could now be shaded between melody and accompaniment, hitherto an impossibility, even on a harpsichord with two keyboards. In the slow movement of the Sonata in E flat major (No 52) of Haydn, a new expressive quality could be realised:

Similarly a balance similar to that of second violins accompanying firsts could be obtained in the slow movement of the Mozart Sonata in F Major (K 332):

By the time of John Field (1782–1837) this type of writing had developed into singer and accompaniment, the melody floating over a wash of sound which did not aim at any independence, but was content to fill in the harmony over pivotal bass notes sustained by the pedal:

Pedalling played an important part in Beethoven's piano-music, but his indications are no longer wholly valid on the modern piano. Tactful half-pedals can be inserted in the following passage from the first movement of the Sonata in D minor, Op. 31, No. 2, while maintaining the overall effect of cave-like mystery, making sure the pedal is never completely released:

The exact observance of his pedal markings in the second movement of the Concerto No. 3 in C minor is unacceptable to our ears, on our infinitely more powerful piano. Here again discreet half-pedals minimize the clash of harmonies which there is on the contemporary grand, while retaining the 'other world' feeling Beethoven expresses here. His markings later in the movement are very effective on our piano, 'senza sordini', with the sustaining pedal, and 'con sordini', without it:

It is curious that Beethoven's sonatas up to Op. 79 ('alla tedesca' in G major) were published as being for piano or harpsichord, when they are obviously written for the piano. The first movement of the 'Moonlight' Sonata would be impossible, the last movement unthinkable, on the harpsichord. Beethoven would have appreciated the power of the contemporary piano, although he would miss the fine pianissimo which was possible by the shifting to one string on some of the pianos of his day. He preferred the depth of the English or German actions to the light touch of the Viennese instruments. The strings of a wooden-framed piano could not stand up to his energetic poundings, which may have been induced by his deafness. Probably he would have sympathized with the celebrated English woman pianist who, on trying a restored Broadwood piano of his day, asked: 'How do you get it louder?'

Liszt's Petrarchan Sonnets were published by Haslinger in Vienna in 1846 as being for 'clavicembalo' (harpsichord), which must have been a mistake. The lighter touch of the pianos of Chopin's day must have made his études less physically demanding than on our piano. Brahms had the advantage of the iron-frame for his massive, deep-set style.

The late nineteenth century piano was still a sufficiently delicate instrument for Debussy's subtle imaginings of ruined temples by moonlight, reflections of clouds and trees in a lake, of a Corot-like stillness, or goldfish flashing in a bowl. The lighter action of a French piano suits his music more than a German grand. Like Chopin, Debussy preferred the more sensitive touch of an upright piano, where his desired illusion of the piano having no hammers is easier to create. A true Debussy sound is difficult to evoke and rarely heard on the contemporary piano. It was easier to suggest on a pre-1939 piano, and Vladimir Horowitz, always a pianist with marvellous tone-colour, produced magical sounds in the Etudes and the *Serenade for the Doll*. Alfred Cortot and Walter Gieseking were unmatched in Debussy; Maggie Teyte and Alfred Cortot have left us the Debussy songs on record in performances of exquisite sensitivity. Ravel's tone-palette needs a very precisely regulated piano, particularly in *Gaspard de la Nuit*. Rachmaninov's virile virtuosity needs all the power of which a piano is capable, but a pre-1939 piano gives more charm to his soaring melodies.

Recently the piano has been composed for in an intellectual style which avoids its more ingratiating pianistic qualities. Here the contemporary piano comes into its own. Singing qualities are not called for, nor easily obtainable from the present piano, whose objectivity is eminently suitable for percussive music. A dramatic work like Michael Tippett's Second Sonata (1962) emerges in bold outlines, for which the contemporary piano is ideal, the only piano to do justice to this strong work of musical mosaic, its angry clashings followed by stark silences. It is amusing that the composer refers to it as a 'little work'. For the pianist it is hardly that, but little in the sense that it lasts only eleven minutes. It is a tense drama of majestic Greek tragedy deriving from its composer's opera *King Priam*. A technical challenge to any pianist, it is among the grittiest and strongest English piano works, and needs an equally iron piano for its full realization. The piano works of Stockhausen and Boulez also need a strongly-resistant piano for the assault on the instrument which they demand.

CHAPTER 4

SOME FAMOUS PIANISTS

Pianism has latterly become a matter-of-fact, mechanical pursuit. All that now appears necessary are hands and a spinal chord, where head, heart, nerves, personality, breadth of musicianship and cultural background used to be involved.

I once asked Edwin Fischer why there were no more artists of the calibre of Paderewski or de Pachmann. 'You only have to look at their faces,' was his reply. Certainly it is rare to find in our day a pianist with the aura which surrounds a great man, or who gives the impression of an exceptional person. Compare the photographs of great pianistic personalities of the past with the famous ones of the present time. The dedicated artist with a face of some spirituality has been replaced by the impersonal image of a passport photo. Today's pianist uses up many passports in the course of the easy communications provided for him by air travel. Famous pianists once looked like musicians and played as such, but now they often look like bank managers and play with the impersonality of computers.

In this book, which is primarily concerned with piano playing, it is impossible to discuss all the famous international pianists of the present time. I mention only five of the most outstanding. The curious thing is that one's keenest musical pleasures often come from quite unknown pianists, particularly in Eastern Europe, whose artists may be unknown in the West. Often the famous will disappoint you with perfunctory readings of works. Perhaps there is a tendency for them to become routined with the constant repetition of their programmes.

Elsewhere I have drawn attention to the superlative pianistic qualities of Vladimir Horowitz, who remains unchallenged in our time. The beautiful sounds he draws from the instrument, his application of tone-colour and his phenomenal technique give his playing a distinction not attained by anyone else. As someone remarked after one of his last London concerts: 'All the pianists were there, wringing their hands'. Horowitz's career which began very early, and his development as a pianist, would make a very interesting psychological study in itself. His playing has undergone marked changes, brought about by illness and change of environment from Europe to America.

Claudio Arrau is a very fine artist who plays with an obvious love for music. His approach is essentially Latin, and his playing has a marvellous translucence which is most suitable to Latin music. Light and colour are his special virtues; Ravel's *Ondine* glistens under his fingers. I have also heard him give an absorbing, scholarly account of the Beethoven Diabelli Variations. It is in the Teutonic Romantic composers that his tone seems wrong. Latin clarity is not enough for Brahms and Schumann; more Germanic thrust is desirable.

Arthur Rubinstein, the doyen of pianists, can fill any hall anywhere in the world by virtue of the legend which has attached itself to his seniority. Tireless energy was once a feature of his playing with a buoyant virtuosity which was always stimulating to hear. Now, alas, he sometimes sounds cold and impersonal, possibly, because his strength seems to be declining.

Sviatoslav Richter, whose reputation was legendary long before he ever played in the West, is an unpredictable pianist. In music with which he has temperamental affinity, the Chopin F minor Ballade or the Rachmaninov F sharp minor concerto Opus 1, for example, he carries all before him; otherwise he can often play coldly. Efficiency and precision are not enough.

A player who eschews romanticism, in common with

present-day pianists and pianos, is Arturo Benedetti Michelangeli. Yet there are few pianists who have his command of the keyboard in range of technique and tone-colour. The trouble with contemporary pianism is that it seems primarily concerned with digital dexterity.

We miss a Schnabel to interpret Beethoven, a Cortot to play Chopin and Schumann, a Fischer to expound Bach. None of these players would be considered technically brilliant or particularly accurate at the present time, but their type of artistry is sadly lacking among our pianists. And can we match the playing of Sergei Rachmaninov? Earlier audiences who heard Paderewski, Busoni, Rubinstein and Liszt realised they were in the presence of great men. Present-day pianists rarely give this impression.

CHAPTER 5

THE CONTEMPORARY PIANIST

Franz Liszt, the founder of the solo piano recital, was by all accounts the first and last great pianist. 'Where Liszt appears, all other pianists disappear,' was W. Von Lenz's comment in *Great Piano Virtuosos* (Schirmer, 1899). This was the judgment of a man who heard all the great pianists of his time, who, as a young man studied with Chopin and Liszt, and who knew Tausig, Field, Moscheles, Kalkbrenner and Henselt and it seems also to have been the general opinion in the nineteenth century. One only has to examine Liszt's compositions to realize the quality of his virtuosity. Others may have written difficult works in a more complicated unpianistic way: Liszt remains to this day the unchallenged master of technical brilliance for the piano. He was born in the era of the wooden-framed piano, but saw its development through its most exciting stages in France and Germany, congratulating the firm of Steinway in Hamburg on the power of their iron-framed grand of the 1880s, a few years before his death.

Until Liszt's time, concerts were usually given by a number of performers, vocal and instrumental, but his magnetic personality and dynamic pianism established the precedent of the solo performer in a way that has not been emulated since. He was a born showman. His concerts appear to have been more informal then ours, his programmes sometimes adapted to suit the tastes of his audience on the spur of the moment. He would improvise on themes submitted to him, a practice which sometimes survives in our time in organ recitals, or in the fragmentary improvisatory preludes which Rachmaninov, for instance, might make to a concert. Now a recital has become such a serious cut-and-dried professional routine that an audience would probably think something had gone amiss if a pianist indulged in any flights of fancy. Spontaneity and individuality are not encouraged today. We take our piano recitals very seriously indeed.

The very word 'recital' was apparently used for the first time to describe a concert given by Liszt in London in 1840. Following in his train were dozens of pupils who flocked to him from all over the world, among them his future son-in-law Hans von Bülow, the Scotsman Eugen d' Albert and the brilliant Carl Tausig, who died at the age of twenty-nine. Like their master, the greatest of Liszt's pupils were not only experts of prestidigitation, but musicians of wide cultural and musical interests—composers, conductors and teachers. This breadth of outlook was characteristic of many nineteenth century piano virtuosi, whose music-making was much more than clever piano-playing. Wholly dedicated, they expressed their lives through their music, regarding the piano as only one branch of music, which in turn belonged to art as a whole.

Anton Rubinstein, esteemed next to Liszt as a pianist, founded the St. Petersburg Conservatoire in 1862. His brother Nicolas established a similar institution in Moscow two years later. These were the beginnings of a great Russian school of piano-playing which has lasted until today. The celebrated teacher Theodor Leschetitzky taught at the St. Petersburg Conservatoire for eighteen years before settling in Vienna, where his fame became world-wide after the success of his pupil Ignace Paderewski. Though independent of Liszt, the Rubinsteins or Leschetitzky, Ferruccio Busoni and Leopold Godowsky were nevertheless of the same giant stature.

In the twentieth century this breadth of outlook, the 'grand manner', has gradually dwindled away, leaving the pianist usually restricted to the piano, in accordance with a narrow world of specialization—not a musician with a

Franz Liszt.

Ignacy Paderewski plays the Minuet, painting by Charles
E. Chambers.

Ignaz Friedman.

Vladimir Horowitz.

large view of music, but a 'commercial traveller' or professional, playing the piano to a large audience. Some, who
had roots in the nineteenth century, whose horizons extended beyond the piano lid, like Sergei Rachmaninov, Arthur
Schnabel, Alfred Cortot or Edwin Fischer, still took a
universal, humanistic view of their art. Present day pianists
are usually shy of showing their feelings, preferring to
'play it cool'.

Rachmaninov the composer is beginning to be appreciated, whereas formerly it was his superlative piano-playing
that commanded greater respect. Among the huge output
of his composition the Prelude in C sharp minor and the
second Piano Concerto were regarded as his most significant
works, while the other twenty three preludes and three
piano concertos were neglected, the songs, orchestral
works and symphonies almost ignored. Now the tide has
turned. Works like the Isle of the Dead and the three
Symphonies have come into their own. In the second
Symphony Rachmaninov seems to have found the most perfect expression of what he was trying to say in the piano concertos. The colourful scoring has no need of any distracting
virtuosity from the piano; it has an extraordinary unity,
a thread running through its texture like that of the third
Piano Concerto. But it has not the occasional longueurs
of the Concertos; every note has meaning in relation to the
whole from beginning to end.

Apart from his astounding virtuosity at the keyboard,
Rachmaninov had a composer's peculiarly penetrating
insight into the works he played. In the tradition of the
great nineteenth century pianists, he found wider expression
as a conductor.

Alfred Cortot as a young man was a répétiteur at Bayreuth. In his conducting the same spiritual quality of his
playing was evident. Radio Suisse-Romande broadcast
in 1967 a recording they had made some years previously,
when Cortot conducted the Suisse-Romande orchestra
in a performance of the Franck Variations Symphoniques,
with a pupil as soloist. This work had been one of his great
interpretations as a pianist, and it was rare to hear the
orchestral score conducted with such sensitivity. Cortot

can be heard on gramophone records as a conductor in collaboration with Jacques Thibaud and Pablo Casals, with whom he also played some memorable chamber music.

Edwin Fischer too looked beyond piano playing. For some years he conducted an orchestra at Baden Baden, and quite often revived the eighteenth century custom of directing Bach and Mozart concertos from the keyboard. Artur Schnabel was a keen thinker, and a composer, as yet unknown. Like these others, with the exception of Rachmaninov, he was a great teacher, and interested in the discerning musician's world of chamber music.

We have no longer outstanding teachers of the stamp of Leschetitzky, or his later English counterpart Tobias Matthay, who were as dedicated as any performer. Perhaps such figures appear very seldom. The present-day gifted piano student has not even the choice of teachers of his pre-second World War counterparts—Egon Petri, Schnabel, Cortot, Friedman or Fischer, to name but a few.

There may have been fewer pianists in the nineteenth century than now, but there were many great artists among them. Now pianists are legion, and their standard of technical efficiency is very high indeed. Piano-playing has become an accomplishment not hard to master with a little talent and much application. It seems not so much a calling as an available career, and young pianists acquire facility in the way that a typist learns to type at speed. They compete in international competitions which are held in more and more countries every year, which put emphasis on technique. From these contests the winners are launched into the concert-hall where some of them continue to play as if they were still in an international competition (as indeed they are, of another kind). Each year the average age of pianists before the public becomes less.

It is a characteristic of the young pianist at the present time that he plays brilliantly, noisily and superficially. The day of the specialist in the more attractive qualities of the instrument, who took delight in beautiful sound, seems to be over. Perhaps the sound is no longer there to be drawn from the piano as it is now constituted, and certainly audiences appear to be dazzled by technical bravura, sacrificing discrimination on the altar of brittle youth.

Since 1945 there has been an enormous expansion in the performance of music through concerts, radio, television and film, which has created a mass audience in contrast with the former few, more musically informed. In 1900 a concert was an event, now it is only one among many musical manifestations in the major capital cities of the world every night. Musical festivals have become annual presentations for which the organizers must find programmes; radios broadcast music incessantly, recording companies compile an annual schedule. More students enter colleges of music, and more and more pianists are born into a world of mass-production where cold efficiency, professionalism and uniformity seem to count most.

Women pianists seem to outnumber men in the proportion of 3 to 1 possibly because piano-playing is considered a domestic accomplishment more suited to the female. They certainly play the piano more nimbly than their male colleagues, but their suppleness of finger is not always matched by an equal perceptivity of touch. Generally a man has more clarity in articulation, more sensitivity in his finger-tips. As women are supposed to be the weaker sex, they appear to try to overcome this defect at times by attacking the piano with more force than men, not always to musical effect. In our time we have heard some remarkably brilliant women pianists, notably the Australian, Eileen Joyce. Tobias Matthay had a famous trio of sensitive artists in his pupils Myra Hess, Irene Scharrer and Harriet Cohen.

It takes almost as many people to launch a pianist on the concert platform, as it does to support a soldier in the front line. Most important of these unseen supporters is the piano-maker, on whose skill the pianist relies. To keep up with an ever-expanding market, piano construction is no longer a personal occupation, but a factory job. Pianos are produced in large quantities but surprisingly enough retain individual characteristics, as no six instruments from one maker at the same time seem alike in touch and tone. Under different acoustic conditions, a piano sounds and feels different to the player, and in spite of an age of 'planning' it is rare to find a new hall which is accoustically satisfactory for a piano recital.

Responsibility for the care and maintenance of a piano lies with the tuner and the regulator. One person who combines both skills is seldom found, and at present the standard of tuning is higher than that of regulation, an ability only acquired over a long period. After the piano manufacturer the regulator is the pianist's most important ally. He can change the weight of the keys, and the disposition of their weight, which affects depth of touch. He can also change a piano's tone by the 'voicing' of an instrument, treating the felt hammer-heads to make it rounder or brighter as required. Before 1939 the trend was for mellow tone and shallow action; now the fashion has shifted to bright sound and a deep touch.

It is this action, or 'feel' of the piano keyboard which is all important to the player, and the success of his performance will largely depend on whether he is comfortable with it. Different pianists naturally like different pianos, different kinds of actions. At the present time piano keys are usually heavy, weighing 47 to 50 grammes, prepared with a deep action to give the player more striking power. It is interesting that the very few pianists who permit themselves the luxury of travelling with their own pianos, have the action lightened almost to a feather-weight touch, while the tone is kept mellow. The majority of players however have to be content with what pianos are provided for them, and naturally it is impossible for a concert-hall to maintain pianos at a level of tone and touch to suit all performers. An audience is quite often unaware with what a pianist may be contending when playing on an uncongenial instrument.

Whereas the eighteenth century harpsichordist had to be able to tune his instrument, which never held its pitch for long, a pianist nowadays is only concerned with the outside of his piano, leaving the inside to the specialists. It is a pity that pianists are not made more conscious of the piano's mechanism during their student days, as it would help them in specifying their needs when a piano is being prepared for a concert.

With the expansion of audiences piano recitals are now

often held in halls far too big for the instrument. Von Lenz quotes Meyerbeer: 'The piano is intended for delicate shading, for the cantilena, it is an instrument for close intimacy.' This attitude finds little favour today. Before 1939 the piano was heard to advantage in halls of modest size. After the first World War a pianist of the stature of Ferruccio Busoni was still content to play in the Bechstein (now Wigmore) Hall on his return to London, and the greatest pianists continued to be heard there between the two wars. After 1945 they often moved to larger halls which defeated the piano's intimacy, and demanded an extrovert athletic style of playing. Pianists of the type of Malcuzynski and Julius Katchen readily supplied this, and needed a piano strong enough to withstand their boxer-like assaults.

Not everyone followed the new style of playing or liked the new piano. 'Older pianists like old pianos,' Stefan Askenase is reported to have said in Berlin. The post-war recital's large audience made it a worthwhile commercial proposition, but musically the large hall defeated the piano's finer sensibilities—though it cannot be said that this seemed to worry the 'cash pianists'.

Growth of communications has opened up music in many parts of the world which formerly saw the inter-national artist very seldom. Tropical countries present special problems, particularly as regards the piano, which is hard to maintain in good order in hot and humid condi-tions. If good regulators are scarce in the world centres of music, it can be imagined how rare they are in remote areas. Pianos destined for hot countries usually undergo a process of 'tropicalization' before they leave Europe. Strings are plated to make them rustless, the soundboards screwed down, felts are sewn as well as stuck, bushings are pinned as well as glued. In spite of these precautions 'tropicalized' pianos may still be difficult to play in unsuitable climatic conditions, owing to the lack of expert maintenance. Their tone may also be affected by the treatment of the strings to prevent rusting.

Amid all these varying conditions of pianos, halls and climate, the pianist has only his sense of duty to guide him to make the best of his varying circumstances. He is more than grateful for a well-maintained piano with a sympathetic action, for a hall whose acoustics suit his instrument. In his search for stylistic truth he endeavours to make acceptable the mammoth grand which must substitute for so many earlier instruments, neither underplaying its natural sonority, nor over-inflating music written for weaker-toned pianos with which it has little in common.

Since Van Cliburn won the Tchaikovsky competition in Moscow in 1953, and was catapulted into stardom overnight, international piano contests have become increasingly more important to the aspiring young pianist. Here was the phenomenon of an American winning first prize in Russia, a stronghold of twentieth century pianism. It was 'news', and as such was much publicized in America.

International competitions are not new; many distinguished pianists have won European honours in them in the past, among them Michelangeli, Emil Gilels, Moura Lympany and Lance Dossor. With greater prominence in the press and magazines, and a wide coverage on television screens throughout the world, they now receive far more publicity than formerly and have become more like musical Olympic Games. The limelight now falls on those held in Moscow and Leeds, which have eclipsed the more dignified jousts in Geneva and Paris.

Musical contests are not new. In the nineteenth century one player might compete with another in public. Many pianists of different nationalities playing against one another in practically every European country and in America is a twentieth century novelty. The victor is usually the most competent technician. The attraction for the ambitious young pianist lies in the television and recording contracts, the engagements offered to the winner, the spotlight of world publicity, which will make him famous overnight. As these competitions are held annually, a crop of new young pianists appear on the concert scene each year. As by nature of their youth they are still immature artists, they do not always make for very interesting listening on the concert platform.

The young pianist is not new, but the emphasis on the

young player is a new feature of our concert life. Precocious talent has always been exciting to hear, but it needs time to mature, alongside mature artists. Some concert agents exploit this idea of the young pianist, in the manner of pop-star promoters.

These young pianists certainly have clever fingers. Nothing daunts them. In their post-student years they perform astonishing feats: the Hans Werner Henze Second Piano Concerto (Christoph Eschenbach), the complete Beethoven Sonatas (Daniel Barenboim), the complete Mozart Concertos (Stephen Bishop), the complete Scriabine Sonatas (John Ogdon). The latter's repertoire seems to be boundless, including, for example, works of Messiaen (*Vingt régards sur l'Enfant Jésus*) and Busoni (Concerto).

Playing the piano is not merely a matter of accuracy and speed however; it is also concerned with individual personality and expression. Too many of these young pianists seem cast from the same mould, turned out from the same production-line. John Lill, a fêted Moscow prize-winner, will play you a meticulous Brahms-Händel Variations and Fugue, fabulous in its accuracy and precision, but with little conviction or involvement in the music.

Alfred Brendel, serious and scholarly, obviously takes care over stylistic problems, particularly textural ones. Bruno Leonardo Gelber, seems to have far more musical commitment than many of his contemporaries, but even he can fall victim to the commonest complaint of the contemporary pianist, excessive speed. In an otherwise splendid performance of the Schumann Concerto, he spoils the last movement by taking it at an unusually and unstylistically fast tempo.

Never mind that Beethoven wrote his Op.111 after a long evolutionary spiritual process, in the years of maturity, when he had left the world behind. The latest young pianist will be ready to perform it for you. Perhaps the next stage in this trend will be the teenage pianist, or the child of five, essaying the Diabelli Variations. Contemporary youth does not hesitate to don the mantle of age in its pianistic searchings; unfortunately there is no short cut to the experience and wisdom which should accompany it. These cannot be bought cheaply or assumed, without cost, except through the passage of time.

The young pianists of today give us far too much glib, superficial playing. They are too stereotyped, and lack any 'grand manner' in their presentations.

CHAPTER 6

NEW MEDIA FOR THE PIANIST

The contemporary pianist has new media open to him undreamt of by Liszt, who no doubt would have entered into them with his characteristic zest, although missing the personal contact with an audience which was so necessary to him. He might not have enjoyed the mechanical reproduction of the piano, which robs a live performance of a good deal of its vitality, and takes away freshness and delight from our listening. What can be obtained casually on gramophone record or radio, we treat casually, using it so often as a comforting background noise.

Of the new artificial forms which involve the pianist, the film commands most attention, because, like a concert, it requires participation on our part. A biographical film about a musician is not very rewarding to the seeker after musical truth. If reality were maintained and some verisimilitude to a composer's character and life observed, then it would be an extension of our appreciation of him. One might have more confidence in Hollywood film-makers, if they employed suitable actors or had themselves some musical background, when they embark on musicians' lives. So often a film about a musician is sentimental and vulgar.

Fortunately not all films involving musicians have been tasteless. Around a slight story, a visual record of Paderewski's playing was made in 'Moonlight Sonata' which did not cheapen his art or personality, but was very moving

51

in the way it showed the nobility of the man and the musician. Heifetz also made a welcome appearance on the screen Sometimes pianists have been heard but not seen in films, notably the pianist Claude Frank, whose beautiful playing of haunting pieces by Erik Satie in the film '*Feu Follet*' added greatly to its atmosphere of decadence and hopelessness. A dramatic use of silence too was made in this film, as important to the background as music, a fact which Japanese film-makers have realized to telling effect.

The television camera has invaded the concert hall, a contemporary pianist being willing to put up with the distraction of bright lighting and heat, for the sake of the added publicity. The presentation of piano music on television poses many problems for producers. A telecast of a piano concerto is easier, as the camera gives variety by moving among the orchestra, or concentrating on the camera-conscious conductor putting on special antics for the viewers; they get a better all-round look at him than his concert audience. With his mannerisms cruelly exposed at close range, television is a devastatingly frank medium for a pianist. The sound of the piano is usually so boxed up that one is more conscious of seeing than hearing, the opposite emphasis to the concert-hall, where one is lucky to see at all. Those whose jaws move compulsively as though they are conducting a colloquy with an invisible being, or who roll about like ships at sea, are asking for derision from the unseen audience who are primarily viewers, and not necessarily a captivated listening public. Again it was Mr. Horowitz who gave the most perfect of television presentations, to an invited audience in Carnegie Hall in 1968. Nothing was left to chance in making this masterful film; tests (so important for the pianist) were made, two concerts given, and a composite film put together. Horowitz's style of presentation, like that of Michelangeli, is a model to pianists. He sits quietly at the piano and does not deflect attention from the music by distracting movements. This recital was also happily free from any audience intrusion by the camera. There are few pianists who can hold the attention so absorbingly, and the unity between man and piano was incredible. His playing and personality were such that one forgot the physical materials of ivory, wood, iron and wire which constitute the solid mass of the grand piano. He managed to convey on a television screen that rare intimacy of expression for which the piano used to be valued, and for once the recorded sound was excellent Through television Horowitz can now be seen and heard in countries which are denied his presence, following his retirement from touring.

Studio performance of piano music without an audience is more difficult. Some special presentation is needed; the music is better introduced to the listener by an interesting commentary, either by the performer, or someone qualified to make it. Visually it is not enough to have the one profile view as in the concert hall, and shots of the player from unfamiliar angles add an interest, that can never be experienced at a concert. Sometimes the camera will catch a view of the piano's interior, giving some idea of its mass of taut strings and iron bracings. Choice of programme is all-important, variety of composer and shortness of item being the most suitable. It is not an easy medium for the musician, who in the physical discomfort of hot, moving cameras finds concentration on the music difficult. The critical viewer ensconced comfortably in his armchair has no idea of what a pianist may be enduring on his behalf.

Recording and radio have been invaluable to musical appreciation, extending our knowledge of works and performances that we might otherwise never have had the opportunity to hear. From the days of the pre-electric recordings at the turn of the century, through the period of 78 r.p.m. electrically made discs to the long-playing records of 1950 is a swift technical development in fifty years. A writer in the *Musical Times* of November 1887 asked prophetically, 'Will Rubinstein or little Hofmann make a tour of the world by phonogram, sitting quietly at home and preparing new specimens, while agents travel about displaying them?' In the 1960s this is precisely what Vladimir Horowitz did.

With the advent of stereo recording, an enormous advance in technique has been made, and the powerful piano of the present is ideal for it. It is not surprising that a music-lover may prefer his record collection in the peace of his own home to actual concerts. But recording is not a complete substitute for live performance. There is a sense of collective sharing between performer and audience which is impossible to achieve on an impersonal gramophone. The new method of tape recording has made possible absolute accuracy of notes. Wrong notes had to stay in 78 r.p.m. records, as no editor's sleight-of-hand availed in the case of faulty recording on to a master disc. Now what appears to be a faultless performance, may be the result of a careful synthesis of several, and a standard of accuracy is attainable which is rarely achieved in the concert hall. The smallest slip which may be hardly detected in a recital, stands out on a record. Therefore the editor snips it out of the tape, joining up a correct version.

Tape recording, so easily done in the home, is of incalculable value to the pianist. Listening to one's playing on tape is to hear it as a critical outsider, and many surprises, even shocks, are experienced in the process. Records of others are helpful too, but not to the extent of copying their ideas, which kills spontaneity and individuality. There is no point in giving a carbon copy of another's performance; to do this only implies a lack of conviction on the part of the imitator.

Records help the musician in building up an idea of a composer's style, through hearing as much of his music as possible. Where they can be misleading is in matters of balance. A recording of a piano concerto for example always favours the piano, and gives a false idea of concert conditions, causing some disappointment to a concert-goer familiar with the gramophone version. Unable to judge whether a performance is stylistic because of a superficial knowledge gained through recordings some people are inclined to set themselves up falsely as authorities on music. It is well to remember that although about five hundred new records are issued every month they are only a small part of musical performance as a whole.

The expansion of the market since the advent of the long-playing record has meant that many artists are now heard on disc where formerly it was the privilege of a select few. Not all pianists give the impression that they record as well as they play in public, because of the additional nervous strain of the demon of accuracy, and the elimination of the performer's personality. When so much vitality is lost in the transference from reality to disc, pianists rarely make a recording sound as though they were in the room playing for you. It is such a trying medium to essay that one is grateful for the projection of any artistic quality at all. A musician is at the mercy of the technical equipment, or the acoustic setting of a recording, which can diminish or augment his impact. In recording there is a wide gulf between listener and player but in the concert hall there is contact, so it is not surprising that a few pianists prefer their concert performances, with the extra stimulus of an audience, to be recorded.

Recording has been invaluable in preserving the playing of pianists in the past, and the sound of the pianos they played on. Miraculous feats have been achieved by engineers in resuscitating performances from pianola rolls, old acoustic and 78 r.p.m. recordings, for the more convenient and acceptable L.P. disc. In their new status they are much more enjoyable than they were. A particularly rewarding anthology comes from Warsaw, 'Golden Pages of Polish Pianistic art' consisting of old records of Paderewski, Friedman, Godowsky, Levitzki, Hofmann and others. No greater tribute to a wonderful school of piano playing can be imagined, and it would be impossible to assemble on record a comparable collection of Polish artists of our time. There is nothing more impressive in it than the Chopin E flat major Nocturne Op. 55 played by Ignaz Friedman with a singing tone that could not be produced on today's piano by today's pianist. This is a distillation of a wonderful era of piano playing, when graciousness of touch still counted. Mischa Levitzki, younger than the others, was one of the last of the bon viveurs of the piano, those who savoured and enjoyed the magical sounds which can be produced from it. Not that these pianists were insensible to their instrument's masculine qualities. On the contrary, their playing had wonderful breadth in bigger works. But they did not slaughter the piano as though they hated its inside. Their big playing was not smashed down from above the keys, but hands were kept close to them. To hear players in our time like Mieclaw Horzowski or Paul Baumgartner, who are steeped in this tradition, is a rare joy. There is also a Chopin album of Ignaz Friedman taken from pianola rolls he made in America in the 1920s, which have been transferred to an L.P. He might be back playing for us. There is an elasticity, a rubato, which is eschewed by the literal-minded contemporary pianist, in a performance of the F minor Ballade. What characterizes these pianists apart from their musicality and fine touch, is the clarity of their finger-technique. The claims that are made for the superiority of the contemporary pianist's technique vanish before the performances of the Chopin G sharp minor Study in thirds by Moritz Rosenthal, or the Strauss-Schulz—Evler Blue Danube Arabesques by Emil Sauer. And it is not mere technique; every note fits in to a musical pattern of sound. Could these players have played like this on today's piano?

Early twentieth century pianists did not hesitate to add notes or alter the text at times, if they felt justified. This was not new. Liszt would make changes or add embellishments to a piece, if he felt they improved it, for to him nothing was sacred. As Chopin said, he dared all. Free ornamentation of the printed notes where appropriate was not unusual in his day, as a legacy from the graceful eighteenth century. We tend to be more conservative now, regarding a score as sacrosanct. If the older virtuosi considered a passage badly written, they did not hesitate to alter it. Doubling of left hand notes with the octave below, adding notes or altering the ending of a piece were all regarded as acceptable practices. It was the fashion of its time, an exuberance from the joy of playing.

Listen to the 'Minute' Waltz of Chopin in their hands. This poor plaything of pianists was tossed about with reckless abandon. Its superfluous nickname was given to it by speed-merchants who aimed at flying through it in sixty seconds flat, which makes nonsense of it musically. Even the fleet-fingered Friedman resisted the temptation to rush it off its feet. His recording of it reads 'Minute Waltz—Time 1 minute 30 seconds'. But nobody could leave its notes alone, Pachmann, Friedman, Rosenthal or Godowsky—each did something different, superimposed double thirds, interpolat-

ed counter-melodies, or added some flourishes at the end.
Usually these high spirits were only applied to trifles like
this waltz. But a hyper-sensitive artist such as Alfred Cortot
did not refrain from changing the last chords of the Chopin F
minor Fantasy, or the B minor Sonata. Sometimes these
changes sound unnecessary to our ears. Yet, contemporary report had it that Chopin never played a piece
the same way twice. How he would shock today's critics
who reprove pianists when they alter dynamic markings
in a score.

Reproduction of the piano in radio studio recitals, or
broadcasts of pianists from concert halls never seem to
reach the standard of gramophone recordings. Like television a boxlike sound is inevitable. A radio piano recital
sometimes has the acoustic effect of an empty swimming-
bath. Eighteenth century piano works usually broadcast
well because of the scarcity of sustaining-pedal, and the
light texture of the music. Big romantic works are less
successful. But the radio station's greatest difficulty is in the
maintenance of its pianos, which are in continual use, and
sometimes cared for in a perfunctory manner.

Radio has tremendous power in improving musical
taste, and developing our sense of style. In a civilized
community it should not be presumptuous to expect serious
music to be available at all times, to balance the surfeit
of 'pop'. This unfortunately is not always the case but the
balance has been partially redressed in England by the
advent of Radio 3, Radio-diffusion Française has a magnificent programme of classical recorded music throughout
the day, but unfortunately it does not seem to be available
outside France. Even on short-wave, pop is loudly predomi-
nant, serious music a faint exception. A coverage of all
kinds of music with an extremely high standard of performance in live and recorded presentations is provided from
early morning to midnight by Radio Beromünster in
German Switzerland. There are always alternative programmes from French or Italian Swiss stations; in addition
Switzerland is so luckily situated that programmes from her
neighbouring countries of France, Germany, Austria and

Italy are always available. The intelligent Swiss radio listener has a wonderful choice of programmes at his disposal, even those of the surrounding countries being fully documented in his radio journal.

CHAPTER 7

STYLE AND NATIONALITY

A composer's style is closely linked with his nationality, his country's attitude to music, its aptitude for it. A young musician growing up in the environment of Vienna, for example, cannot help absorbing some of the musical tradition which surrounds him. He hears the angelic voices of the Vienna Boys' Choir, and proudly remembers that Haydn and Schubert were once choristers in his city. He goes to the opera, listens to the golden string tone of the Vienna Philharmonic Orchestra, both conducted at one time by Gustav Mahler. Statues erected to honour great composers of the past remind him that adopted Viennese like Beethoven and Brahms left their native Bonn and Hamburg in favour of his city, which ranked with Paris and Rome as one of the artistic capitals of the world. If he is a piano student he practises studies by Beethoven's pupil Carl Czerny, whose method opened up a new field of piano technique, still valid for pianists today. All the great pianists of the past came to play in Vienna; some spent their formative years there as pupils of Leschetitzky. It is the home of the Bösendorfer piano, whose largest model has an exceptional length of 9 feet 6 inches and a compass of 8 octaves. With such a background of beautiful sounds, sights and associations, small wonder the Viennese piano student plays in a careful musicianly style which has respect for the finer qualities of piano touch.

Vienna's proud façade of beautiful buildings and houses

is still there, but behind it is but a memory of the opulence of her Imperial days. Two World Wars, Nazism and Russian occupation have stripped her of her former splendour. There remains however the quiet charm of a city 'whose yesterdays look backwards with a smile through tears.' Averting her gaze from the contemporary musical scene, except in the cafés where there are now juke-boxes as in any other city, Vienna clings nostalgically to her rich past. In a city where some of the most revolutionary aspects of twentieth century composition originated in the atonal and dodecaphonic works of Arnold Schönberg, Anton Webern and Alban Berg, concert programmes are surprisingly conservative. A Viennese audience seems nonplussed by contemporary piano music, preferring its familiar gods of Haydn, Mozart, Beethoven, Schubert and Brahms. It even seems puzzled by a harpsichord.

If Germany has no one city whose historical associations equal those of Vienna—which country has?—from her many thriving musical centres she has given us more great composers than any other nation. Without them our concert life would be very thin indeed. They form the core of our listening, by virtue of their depth of feeling, their intellectual ability to shape satisfyingly logical music, the technical ability to execute their designs. The two greatest of them created living music of the highest structural quality—Bach in fugue, Beethoven in sonata form. A romantic like Brahms still used classical forms; Schumann's ardour overflowed from them. Wagner unleashed an emotional torrent of passionate intensity, for which he created his own appropriate form, the leitmotiv (leading motive) which told its own story. And our musical debt to Germany is not confined to the eighteenth and nineteenth centuries—one of the most significant voices of contemporary composition is that of Hans Werner Henze.

Music is not a dispensable luxury to the Germans, only to be tolerated in times of affluence. It is as essential to them as food and drink. The number of opera-houses in Germany and the priority given to the rebuilding of those destroyed between 1939 and 1945 is evidence enough. Nor was there any superfluous wish to disturb the continuity of musical performance—where the acoustics of a concert hall had been good, it was rebuilt exactly as it had been. Concert and opera-going are not frivolous pastimes in Germany, but occasions taken very seriously as deeply-enjoyable pleasures. A concert there is an experience to be remembered.

Opera, although usually sung in German, whatever its original language, is produced with a great sense of style, German opera singers being well trained as actors. An exception in our time was the wave of perverse productions of his grandfather's music dramas by Wieland Wagner at Bayreuth. These are revived at times in other cities, but in Munich romantic visual beauty is retained for what are essentially romantic works.

The best German orchestras play with a tonal intensity unmatched by any other country, with such unity that the effect is of one, not one hundred, instruments. Only in Germany can one hear truly idiomatic orchestral perfor-mances of Wagner and Strauss, because the German tem-perament has enough hedonism to luxuriate in their magnificence of sound. Orchestral programmes show that Germany is more cognizant of twentieth century music than most other countries, without making any special pleading for it—it simply takes its place naturally and unselfcon-sciously alongside other music.

If a town wishes to buy the best available piano it naturally turns to Germany, whose instruments have developed an unparalleled standard of craftsmanship since the late nineteenth century. German pianos are to be found on concert platforms all over the world because of their superior depth and richness of tone, their brilliance and efficiency of action. It was in the kitchen of his home in Seesen in the Harz mountains that Heinrich Engelhard Steinweg made the first Steinweg, or as it is now known, Steinway piano. Unsatisfied with opportunities in Germany he emigrated to America in 1850, founding the famous Steinway firm in New York in 1853. A branch factory was opened in Hamburg in 1880 which has produced Steinway pianofortes for Europe and overseas countries ever since, in spite of being badly damaged in 1943. Another great piano house whose roots stretch back to the nineteenth century is that of Carl

Bechstein in West Berlin; the Blüthner factory is in Leipzig, in East Germany.

Penetration and seriousness are characteristics of German piano-playing, as we remember from players such as Artur Schnabel and Wilhelm Backhaus. Foreign pianists were attracted to live in Germany; Ferrucio Busoni settled in Berlin, and Liszt after many years in Weimar, finally went to Bayreuth. In the peaceful cemetery there, lie several famous nineteenth century musicians with him, Karl Klindworth and the conductor Hans Richter among them.

Naturally enough the best Beethoven players are German, but the German-Swiss Edwin Fischer, who lived in Germany until 1939, brought a mischievous sense of fun to many a light-hearted Beethoven movement which German pianists in their earnestness, sometimes miss. A genial Mozart movement too is sometimes apt to sound more solidly German than Austrian in the hands of a German pianist.

Whereas Germany has a tradition which goes back at least five hundred years, Russian stringed-keyboard composition and playing are not even two hundred years old, and consist exclusively of piano music. When the Russian court began importing foreign artists from Western Europe in the eighteenth century, the piano came too. The Irish composer-pianist John Field visited St. Petersburg from London to demonstrate Muzio Clementi's pianos in 1803. His success with the aristocracy was such that he was encouraged to settle there. The Russians took quickly to the piano, their natural mobility in artistic expression soon becoming apparent in the virtuosity of their players. Strangely Russia never became particularly interested in making pianos; as in other countries, one finds a German instrument on their concert platforms. Anton Rubinstein, Tchaikovsky and Glazunov wrote brilliant piano music. It did not have the cutting-edge of Liszt's diamond-like style, but was more akin to the sonority of another Slav, Chopin. Nineteenth century Russian playing and composition brought out the piano's liquid qualities; as with Chopin the bass line, supported by the sustaining pedal, was the edifice on which everything else was built. Perhaps this style came naturally to a race of singers. Scriabine and Rachmaninov carried

A Blüthner pianoforte.

A Bechstein piano.

A Börsendorfer piano.

over the Chopin influence into the twentieth century, but in the reaction against romanticism more percussion became evident in the piano writing of Prokofiev, Shostakovich and Khachaturian.

The revolution of 1917 caused as great an upheaval artistically as it did socially. As an émigré, Rachmaninov was forced to live by giving piano recitals in Europe, which distracted him from composition. Asked why he no longer composed, he gave an answer which underlined the melancholy of the exile, 'the melody has gone out of my life.' Rachmaninov's piano writing was more involved, more individual than that of any previous Russian composer, as well as being more pianistic. He shared a Russian love of bell-like sound with Tchaikovsky. The young Horowitz whose playing reached Western Europe in the 1920s, had, like Rachmaninov, astounding virtuosity and even more vitality. Both brought aristocratic bearing to their playing. Before his illness in 1935, it was said that no other living pianist could challenge Horowitz's superiority in that era of exceptionally fine playing. Neville Cardus went one step further when he said he was prepared to believe that he was the greatest pianist 'alive or dead'. His phenomenal playing has had a world-wide influence, particularly on the young.

In Soviet Russia pianistic tradition has been continued, although like their Western counterparts, Soviet pianists play brilliantly, if no longer in the grand manner. Sviatoslav Richter and Emil Gilels have won world acclaim. In Russia, state patronage encourages the best of the younger pianists by making it possible for them to study with the established artists. Thus continuity is assured. Thanks to a thorough system of training and their musical ability, Russian candidates usually win the highest honours in international competitions. Russian orchestral playing is of superb virtuosity, and in Yevgeny Svetlanov they have one of the great conductors of our time. Ballet and theatre, both of great importance to the young musician, are equally fine.

Closely allied with the Russian style of playing is that of Poland, proudly heroic in character, befitting the bravery of a race who have fought for their independence over the centuries. Aristocratic valour shone out in the playing of their greatest pianists, in the seigneurial manner of Paderewski, Friedman and Artur Rubinstein. A country which has produced the most pianistic of composers, Frédéric Chopin, naturally has provided outstanding players too.

French pianism has a particular regard for delicacy, clarity and conciseness. As in Germany it was preceded by a magnificent school of harpsichord playing whose qualities of neatness and finesse continued on the new instrument. French makers made vital developments to the piano in the early nineteenth century, particularly Sebastian Erard and his nephew Pierre. French pianos were lighter in touch than German, and according to von Lenz, the lightest of them made by Ignaz Pleyel and his son Camille, was Chopin's preferred instrument, because 'shading was easier on it than one with a mellower, fuller tone.' French piano writing acquired great technical brilliance in the century through the Lisztian virtuosity of Camille Saint-Saëns. His studies still provide a formidable challenge to the pianist. French pyrotechnics are of a glittering kind similar to that of the French organ-composers of the nineteenth century, though shallow rather than deep in tone. Technical accomplishment, a feature of French piano playing, is based on the thoroughly-planned system of training which their young pianists are obliged to undergo. Oddly enough French women pianists often give a more robust impression than the men, and play with greater fire. The men seem to be more concerned with quality than quantity of tone. Artists mingle in Paris more freely than in most cities—painters, musicians or actors. Their national characteristics of enthusiasm and demonstrativeness are admirable for artistic expression. A series of excellent teachers in Paris has left an impression which has extended beyond the borders of France, particularly on some very gifted South American pianists, notably Bruno-Leonard Gelber, whose sensitive playing shows the influence of the particularly fine pianist, Marguerite Long.

It is curious that the country to whom we owe the invention of the piano should have played so little part in its subsequent development. After its invention in Italy, interest in the piano passed north of the Alps to Germany, Austria, and France, to England and America. Today as in other European countries, German pianos dominate Italian concert platforms. Since the numerous harpsichord sonatas of Domenico Scarlatti there has been no great Italian keyboard composer.

Spain's contribution to piano music has been very colourful, although sometimes a profusion of notes disguises rather slender musical material in the works of her most prolix piano composer, Isaac Albéniz. Enrique Granados and Manuel de Falla were less prodigal of notes, but more imaginative in their disposition of them.

The history of English keyboard composition and playing has unfortunately not been continuous or consistent. Have English musicians lacked confidence in themselves, and the public confidence in them too? Beginning brilliantly in the sixteenth and seventeenth centuries with the virginal composers and Henry Purcell, composition petered out in the eighteenth and nineteenth centuries, not being able to rival any of the great continental figures of these important pianistic years. English keyboard works faded into a polite academism, having nothing original or forceful to say. With the piano works of John Ireland and Arnold Bax signs of life began to appear in the twentieth century, and more vigour has been shown since 1945 in compositions by Michael Tippett and Richard Rodney Bennett.

No specifically English school of piano playing has been established, in spite of the teaching of Tobias Matthay and his pupils. Unlike their continental opposite numbers English students lead a separate rather than a corporate existence. Academies and colleges could do much to improve this by inviting senior English and foreign pianists to give the benefit of their experience in summer master-classes to students. A festival as important as Edinburgh could well invite their principal visiting pianist to take a course of master-classes in the festival weeks.

The English temperament produces a rather reserved type of pianist of cool emotional temperature, even when the player has developed great facility. It is sometimes asked why English entrants do not do consistently well in international competitions. Perhaps the answer is that the teaching at English academies and colleges of music is simply not good enough. Since these institutions were founded in the nineteenth century there has never been enough emphasis on technical training. A few scales at an annual examination are not sufficient. Very rarely are there the specialist piano teachers or practising pianists at these institutions to see that students are properly drilled in the mechanics of their art. Consequently the approach remains largely amateur, students being guided by kindly disposed intelligent teachers whose interest in music is more academic than practical. Where there has been a particularly able teacher, Herbert Fryer for instance, many brilliant pupils have resulted. Perhaps the fashion for imported musicians which began in the eighteenth and continued in the nineteenth and twentieth centuries has disheartened English players.

In deference to British taste for Italian musicians an English composer and lute player John Cooper (born 1570) changed his name to Coprario. In our time Solomon Cutner gained much more prestige with his first name alone. Moura Johnstone has had more appeal to the British public as Moura Lympany. Yet both were no different as pianists for their more attractive foreign sounding professional names.

These peculiarities are not confined to pianists; English conductors are passed over in favour of foreigners when conductors are appointed to English orchestras, subsidized with English taxpayers' money by the Arts Council. Would a Hungarian be invited to captain a British football team? One wonders sometimes when looking at the names of piano soloists engaged by these same government-subsidized orchestras whether there are any British pianists at all. It is surprising that a body as strong as the Musicians' Union does not demand that at least fifty per cent of subsidized orchestral concerts should be given by British conductors and soloists, before their members are allowed to play in them. The actors' union Equity would not allow a similar situation to prevail in the theatre.

A change of attitude on the part of the bureaucratic organizations responsible for musical life in Great Britain could soon remedy this. The B.B.C. are not exactly furthering Britain's musical image abroad by sending their orchestra to other countries with a foreign conductor. One cannot imagine a continental orchestra coming here without a national of its own country at the helm. Has Great Britain no national musical pride? What country would have considered inviting a foreigner to conduct the opening concerts in a hall as important as the Festival Hall in London, when Sir Thomas Beecham was an obvious choice for the occasion?

A national institution like the Promenade Concerts founded by Sir Henry Wood and now controlled by the B.B.C., has become a platform for foreigners at the expense of English musicians. Formerly it was an exciting series which encouraged young unknown performers. Small wonder that the budding English pianist feels himself isolated in an English Academy of Music, anxious about his future when he sees the foreigner encouraged by concert agents, government grants given to organizations who pass over English artists. In these days of planning one more committee might well be formed for the promotion of English musicians.

The continuity of British concert life suffered great disruption as a result of the 1939–45 war. The Queen's Hall, an ideal orchestral hall, ideally situated, was bombed and never rebuilt. In its stead a complex of three new halls has appeared in South London, none of which has been a complete acoustic success. It is not an enjoyable experience to listen to an orchestral concert in the Festival Hall where the accoustics are dry, the appearance not conducive to restful listening. The Elizabeth Hall, mercifully smaller than the Festival Hall, which is far too big for a solo recital, is unsatisfactory acoustically for a solo piano, the Purcell Room impossible for a large concert grand. Other pre-war smaller London recital halls have disappeared, with the exception of the Wigmore Hall, which is badly in need of more comfortable seating and re-decoration. If music had been really valued in Britain after the war, more appropriate steps might have been taken to secure the continuity of musical life. The abrupt change of government put power in the hands of bureaucratic planners who seemed to have little zest for providing adequate substitutes for halls which had been lost.

British piano manufacture which once played such an important role in the development of the instrument has also suffered a sad decline in the twentieth century. There is no reason why this should not be reversed, with more care and assistance on the part of those public bodies who control the fortunes of British music.

Some Commonwealth countries have inherited British inferiority where their own musicians are concerned. The reserved English temperament may give rise to a defect in artistic expression, but at least in a country like Australia this should not be so pronounced. There, even more than in England, resident musicians are continually passed over in favour of foreigners who are brought out to Australia at great cost, and who often are little superior to local artists. A healthy interchange of artists among countries is most desirable. Without it stagnation and isolation would result. When a point is reached, however, where the native musician is automatically regarded as inferior to a visiting foreigner, one wonders just how much further national deprecation can go. What is the point of having conservatoriums and music departments at universities if an Australian is never appointed to conduct an Australian orchestra? Many Australian musicians, singers and pianists among them, are forced to live overseas because they are not given sufficient opportunity to express themselves in their own country.

New Zealand supports her resident artists to a much higher degree, but those responsible for the promotion of chamber music in New Zealand and Australia tend to deny good Australasian chamber music players adequate opportunities to be heard in favour of visitors. More sense of proportion on the part of those responsible for the direction of musical life would result in a more balanced and healthy situation. Piano-making is in its infancy as yet in Australasia, but it shows signs of development.

American piano-playing is vital and brilliant, although its pre-occupation with technical brilliance often seems to be more for its own sake than directed towards musical ends.

It is a brilliance which tends at times to become stereotyped in its extroversion and aggressiveness. Acute stylistic perception is not always evident in a country so far away from the fount of European music, although America has been a refuge for many European musicians uprooted by revolution or political tyranny. But its pianism is extremely efficient, in keeping with the American way of life.

American Conservatories of Music have an admirable system of training their students, and have some fine teachers at their disposal. Always receptive to the new in art, much avant-grade music is being composed in America, and some interesting books on twentieth century music have been written by Americans.

America's contribution towards the piano's progress was notable in its improvements in the first half of the nineteenth century. The founding of the Steinway house in New York gave world-wide impetus to the craft in the second half, continuing up to the present time. Other firms such as Baldwin, and Mason and Hamlin, have also made successful instruments.

CHAPTER 8

A COMPOSER'S STYLE

How often in a picture-gallery have you come across a painting you have never seen before, which produces the glow of recognition of meeting an old friend? You feel you know the picture because you are sufficiently acquainted with the painter's work to be able to identify his style, that individuality of expression which is his alone. But he has certain stylistic characteristics in common with his contemporaries. Even if you cannot name him exactly, you know that he belongs to the French Impressionists, to the Italian Renaissance, or to the Dutch School, as the case may be.

It is the same with music. If you hear a work by chance on the radio, and do not know the composer, provided that he is of sufficient merit to possess an individual style, you should be able to name him, or at least the period to which his work belongs. There are pitfalls here of course, particularly if it is deliberately written in the style of another period, such as Stravinsky writing in his neo-classic vein. There are other problems too; early Beethoven sometimes resembles Mozart or Haydn; an unfamiliar Schubert symphony might be mistaken for a late eighteenth century work by reason of its light texture. The listener who comes upon Heinrich Marschner's opera *Hans Heiling* for the first time, having established that it belongs to the nineteenth century, might be excused for wondering, because of its resemblance to Wagner, whether it is post or pre-Wagnerian.

If a composer is of any worth, the stamp of his style is bound to be imprinted on his music, and sooner or later you will arrive at his identity.

When a visual artist, be he sculptor, painter, furniture-maker or architect, has finished his work, it is there for us to see and evaluate, according to our capacity and knowledge. Nothing that we do to it (apart from the controversial procedures of cleaning and restoring) will alter it in any way. It may represent different things to different people, but it has achieved its being as the creator wished. With music, what is written down is only the beginning. The notes of a score are there to guide us, a blueprint for the realization of the work. But has a musical composition any potentially perfect existence? Did it ever exist absolutely in the mind of the composer? And does what is on paper really represent what he tried to express?

Can we ever hear a perfect realization of a work even if the composer is there to perform or direct it? Might it not be lacking in some quality which causes it to fall short of what he imagined? It is possible too that he may change his view of it after some time, particularly if he is a performer or a conductor. If Chopin could play one of his own pieces differently on different occasions, which was the authentic version? When he heard Liszt play his études, Chopin was delighted because they had a strength he was not able to realize himself. After she had performed one of his piano sonatas, Beethoven told a young lady that she had played it well, but had put something into it he had not imagined during its composition. A performer is often told by a composer that he makes a work sound better than he had written it. 'The world is my idea', wrote Schopenhauer. Is a musical work our idea too, a symphony or a sonata an experience to share with a composer according to our realization of it, whether we are reading the score, playing or listening to it?

With so much creative ability demanding an outlet in composition, one cannot expect composers to be routined performers, although it is a rewarding experience to hear a composer play his own or others' music. Chopin and Debussy had a wonderful perception of the piano's subtlest qualities, but neither of them was fond of public performance. The sight of a large gathering oppressed Chopin, who preferred playing in the more intimate surroundings of a salon, while Debussy considered silence the best way of showing appreciation of a performance. Liszt and Rachmaninov, both phenomenal pianists, did not write music which was as interesting as those who were composers first and indifferent or shy performers second. Perhaps the executant in them overshadowed the composer.

Style of performance being so closely connected with a composer's style of writing, it behoves a performer to identify himself as far as possible with the composer. A helpful way to get to know a composer, and to trace his development, is through a music festival planned around his work. The Munich festivals of the 1950s were particularly useful in the case of Richard Strauss owing to the protagonism of Rudolf Hartmann, Intendant of the Opera at that time. Having been associated with Strauss for many years, he was naturally an authoritative advocate of his work. In a few weeks it was possible to survey the whole span of Strauss's work, from early operas such as *Feuersnot*; the seldom-performed fiercely sensual ballet which he wrote for Diaghilev, *Josephslegende*; the great operas *Die Frau ohne Schatten* and *Der Rosenkavalier*; to the lighter *Capriccio* and *Arabella*, and examples from less known operas, including *Friedenstag*. There was something to be heard from every style and period of Strauss's huge output. Rarely heard orchestral and vocal works were not neglected in a memorial concert on the anniversary of his death, at the end of the festival. Bayreuth performs a similar service to Richard Wagner, and other festivals which concentrate on one composer enlarge our appreciation of him at different stages of his development.

In an evaluation of a composer's style it is not enough for a pianist merely to know his piano-writing. Very few composers have made the piano their chief means of expression, as Chopin did. The pianist who plays J.S. Bach will have much more understanding of him if he is acquainted with his organ, vocal and chamber works, particularly with the sacred works. A knowledge of the symphonies of

Haydn, Mozart and Beethoven is most helpful when essaying their piano sonatas, as many of the processes of their musical thinking are alike in both *genres*, the piano writing sometimes disposed in orchestral style, the formal procedures likewise. Mozart's Sonata in A minor (K 310) is, in its spaciousness, to all intents and purposes, a symphony for piano; the declamatory breadth of its first movement is symphonic. In the slow movement the pianist becomes a singer; obviously a knowledge of the arias of Mozart's operas is a key to stylistic interpretation in this movement. The third movement rounds off the Sonata in the manner of a sympnonic finale.

Familiarity with his late string quartets will help us penetrate into the rarified world of the last five Beethoven piano sonatas. Sometimes there is a direct suggestion of quartet writing, as in the first movement of the Sonata in A major, Op. 101:

Even in the opening bars of such a pianistic sonata as Op. 110 in A flat major there are four parts:

The scherzo of Op. 106 has a similar 4 part movement:

Assai vivace

Chopin's love of opera is evident in many of his song-like nocturnes, with their graceful embellishment in vocal terms, particularly the Nocturne in D flat major Op. 27, no. 2:

Lento sostenuto

It is hard for the pianist to realize Debussy's sensitive tone-palette on the piano unless he has the exquisite orchestral sounds of *La Mer*, *L'aprés-midi d'une Faune*, or *Pelleas et Mélisande* in his ear.

Every composer who has something to say musically, says it in his way as no one else can. Mozart and Haydn as contemporaries shared many things in common—the currently light texture of music, an elegant style of writing, dependence on aristocratic patronage. Yet at no times do their identities merge, Haydn's normally contented writing never reaching the depths of anguish or poignancy of his younger colleague. Chopin, Schumann, Mendelssohn and Liszt, all born within a few years of one another, have attributes of Romanticism in common, particularly the predominance of the emotional content of a work over its form. The piano was their first means of expression. Yet the musical language each used was as different as the Polish, German and Hungarian of their mother tongues, the content of their music as diverse as their natures: Chopin withdrawn, sensitive, melancholy, morbid, yet proud and manly; Schumann a mixture of impetuous warmth and reflective dreaminess, Mendelssohn elegant and charming of manner, Liszt passionately restless, extrovert in his desire for worldly success, yet deeply religious at the same time. Debussy and Ravel, Bax and Ireland are often coupled together, yet each pair has little in common except the harmonic language of their time, so separate are their natures.

Each composer has his own world of sound, according to the age in which he lived, the national characteristics discernible in his style and the type of instrument for which he wrote. In seeking his appropriate quality of touch, a pianist needs a different technique for each.

A pianist who is insensitive to style, uses much the same touch for all composers, regardless of their race or period. To arrive at an appropriate quality of touch eye-witness accounts of a composer's playing can be useful, but several should be read, since reports vary, as we know only too well from the experience of different critics writing on one recital.

It would be refreshing if a present-day virtuoso occasionally emulated early nineteenth century pianists, and played a programme of works written during the last twenty five years, including a fantasia or two of his own on modern operas such as *Peter Grimes* or *The Bassarids*. Not only would this be the most up-to-date kind of piano recital, but it would be one most suited stylistically to the current concert piano.

The different facets of a composer's style are worthy of attention. Too often pianists seem to be thinking 'This is Chopin, so I am going to refine my tone, go into a hot-house mood', drawing a veil of sentimentality over the music, often depriving us of its proudly heroic or masculine qualities, or 'now I'm playing Beethoven so I'm going to be very serious and intense', perhaps spoiling, through misplaced tension, the bubbling good-nature of a work like the first movement of the Sonata in G major Op. 31, no. 1.

Popular misconceptions have grown up around composers through romanticized biography. Perhaps the best way to get to know a composer is through his letters. Here he reveals himself directly, sometimes indiscreetly, writing his own biography, revealing himself as an artist. In the letters of Chopin the image of the weak effeminate composer such as he is sometimes made out to be, disappears in the savage outbursts of 'four-letter words' which have had in translation to be replaced for delicate eyes by asterisks. The letters of Mozart and Beethoven show their outer and inner lives in a way which no biographer can emulate. Correspondence between Wagner and Liszt reveals their close association and musical sympathy. As the romantic biography or film covers his life with a sugary coat of sentimentality, romanticized portraits and ineffectual sculptures encourage a false picture of a composer. A merely factual account of a composer's life is not enough. The successful biography is that which presents his music in relation to the often prosaic details of his existence, but allows him to speak, where possible, about his music, and music in general, in his own words.

In *Poets in a Landscape* Gilbert Highet points out that some creative artists have their gifts highly developed at an early age—in music particularly Mozart, Mendelssohn and Chopin. None of them lived beyond their thirties, and their work scarcely had time to undergo any profound psychological change. Intensity was increased, technique of writing perfected in their maturity, but there was no great development in their style of composition during the span of their short lives. There was more profusion of ideas, a fuller expression in their later works, but fundamentally the characteristics of their earlier compositions persisted, intensified by greater richness and poignancy. Mendelssohn's mercurial faery lightness is as obvious in the last movement of the Violin Concerto (1844) as in the Midsummer Night's Dream, Overture which he composed at the age of seventeen in 1826; Chopin's melancholy as prominent in the Nocturne in E minor which he wrote at nineteen (Op. posth.) as in the Nocturnes of Op. 62. Mozart's sense of poise and structure is evident in the early piano sonatas. In the later ones it is still there, but the later sonatas have expanded and deepened.

Other composers who lived longer, Beethoven, Brahms or Liszt, show a marked difference between their early, middle and late periods of composition. At first, as one might expect, there is youthful exuberance. In the second period comes greater command of virtuosity, expansion of mind and heart. In the later years there is a marked change of style. It would be hard to recognize the flamboyance of the early Liszt in the spare works of his old age. How can one correlate the economy of *En Rêve* (1885) *Richard Wagner Venezia* (1883) or *La Lugubre Gondole* (1882) with the profusion of notes of the Sonata in B minor (1852)? Brahms's piano writing falls into three groups. The last piano pieces of Op. 117, 118 and 119 have an autumnal regret which anticipates Mahler, not to be found in the sunnier set of Op. 76. It is interesting to compare the Sonata in C minor Op. 111 of Beethoven, with his youthful *Sonata Pathetique* in the same key (Op. 13). Both first movements have a solemn introduction but there is as much difference between them as between pathos and tragedy. The thrumming tension of the following Allegro in Op. 13 becomes cosmic despair in Op. 111, the spiritual elevation of its second movement contrasting with the terrestrial conclusion of Op. 13.

Other composers whose lives were shattered by illness, as in the case of Schumann, or exile as with Rachmaninov, had their careers interrupted after a very fruitful beginning. One pleasant exception is Domenico Scarlatti, who apparently wrote the greater number of his delightful sonatas for harpsichord late in life.

CHAPTER 9

STYLE AND PERIOD

Of all aspects of style the most difficult to achieve for the practical performance of music of the last four hundred years is that of period, for with the passing of time conventions have been lost, tastes have changed. We do not even know how the Elizabethan virginalist played the ornaments so freely scattered in his manuscripts, and it was not until the nineteenth century that ornamentation became standard. Meanwhile it varied from country to country, and changed over periods of time as short as fifty years. The pianist who aims at authentic style must be wary to choose idiomatic ornaments which are suitable both to the context of the piece, and to his instrument.

Although most people seem quite happy to accept keyboard music played on a contemporary piano without caring a jot whether it is stylistically appropriate to its period of origin, it may cause disquiet to anyone aware of earlier instruments, earlier conventions and earlier concert-rooms. We would not wish our musicians to deck themselves out in periwigs and knee-breeches for a performance of a Mozart Symphony. We have enough oddities of hair-styles and clothes of our own for future generations to laugh at. It is to the person interested in the appropriate sound that period style matters most.

To hear eighteenth century music played on a twentieth century piano in a large hall is rather like looking at an eighteenth century engraving of a street, and then seeing what a conglomeration of styles it presents today after incongruous nineteenth and twentieth century additions. In the City of London a Christopher Wren church may be hardly noticeable surrounded by ugly Victorian and Edwardian buildings; classic revivals of Greek temples for banks, Gothic for churches; high new office buildings functional rather than beautiful; the ugliness of a railway bridge, whose meaningless outline suggests that progress has not been accompanied by visual beauty. Occasionally as a result of the air-raids in the second World War the Wren Church achieved belated isolation, reminding us of the days when buildings were not allowed to be higher than the roofs of the churches, that their towers might predominate. A similar flash of illumination sometimes occurs in the modern performance of an eighteenth century work, when accumulated stylistic incongruities are stripped away, and like the church, it stands out starkly defined.

But this is rare. Usually we have to be content with the agglomeration of buildings which clutter the original setting. We cannot expect eighteenth century architectural style to last beyond its natural expression. Nor would it have been practical to build in a new style in some other area, although this would have been more harmonious to the eye. Musically, as architecturally, we live in a haphazard mixture of styles. Fortunately musicologists in the twentieth century have investigated stylistic problems of the past, and all musicians owe them a debt of gratitude. But judgment and common sense must be used in the practical application of their findings.

How far a musician is sensitive to stylistic relationships depends of course on his general cultural background. The wider his knowledge of other arts, the more imaginative will be the interpretative approach to his own. To restrict himself to the narrow confines of music does not make for breadth of interpretation or for appreciation of style. It is a pity if his susceptibilities towards the broader cultural implications of his art are not aroused in his student days. 'What are you reading?' was Chopin's question to the young von Lenz at his first interview. Reading is the musician's easiest way of approaching earlier artistic periods. Theatre will quicken his dramatic sense, ballet his rhythmic alertness. Through ballet he will have an opportunity to see some of the dance-forms which he plays—minuet and gavotte, polonaise and mazurka.

Not only do the different brands of music in a given period exhibit related characteristics, but there is an over-all unity between different art-forms in that same era. Its literature drama, painting, music and architecture all have certain stylistic similarities. The freshness of Elizabethan lyric verse is matched musically by the outpouring of madrigals and solo songs. The melodic part of Elizabethan keyboard music gives it its charm, not the variations, which are often crude and uninteresting at an experimental stage of keyboard-writing.

Graceful embellishment was a feature of eighteenth century architecture and furniture; ornamentation was equally lavish in its music. Its literature had a high regard for form, particularly in verse. The eighteenth century garden was essentially formal, balance and neatness being found in all the century's artistic manifestations. Accordingly the construction of musical composition was all important.

By the early nineteenth century, form had become a strait-jacket with which romantic composers became impatient. A new freedom of subject showed itself in the long digressions of the novels of Charles Dickens. Size was a characteristic of romanticism—the fondness for a large canvas in painting, the long novel, the huge symphony or sonata, the lengthy Wagnerian music-drama. Performance expanded, choirs and orchestras grew bigger. It was the period of the large gesture in art, the 'grand manner'. Significantly it was the time of the piano's enlargement in size and volume. However much we may dislike the results, nineteenth century organ-builders who added stops and keyboards to eighteenth century organs were only acting in accordance with the artistic trends of their time.

With our prosaic no-nonsense view of music, we are

inclined to regard earlier music impersonally. The period which suffers most from the outlook is the nineteenth century, whose music will not respond to the contemporary 'play-it-cool' fashion. 'De-romanticizing' nineteenth century works is quite fashionable in our time, in ballet, opera and theatre as well as in piano-playing. The mediaeval legend of Tristan and Iseult, as treated by Richard Wagner breathes romantic passion in music and story. To produce it without appropriately romantic sets, ignoring Wagner's explicit stage directions, is to go against the work's style. It is no excuse to say that a work is 'dated' and must have a new interpreataion in the twentieth century. All works of art are dated in that they belong to the time of their creation. To be realized as fully as possible they need presentation in a manner in keeping with their nature. Otherwise why not abandon production altogether, and have concert perform-ances of opera? The eye is as important as the ear in the theatre or opera-house, but producers are ready to alter, even mutilate the visual in a production, whereas they would not dare to alter a composer's music. Worse still, changes made to ballet or opera productions are not acknow-ledged, and an unsuspecting public imagine they are seeing something authentic.

In order to avoid excessive emotion, pianists often go to the other extreme and play a romantic work as though it had just come out of a 'deep freeze'. They do not alter the score, as a choreographer may alter a ballet, but play down the work's emotional nature, thinking that a busy brilliance of technique will be adequate compensation. Non-involve-ment and detachment do not suit nineteenth century music, any more than the opposite vices of sentimentality or lack of musical coherence. The Greek ideal of the mean, as opposed to the excess or the defect, is desirable here. Some-times in the twentieth century deliberately anti-romantic music has been written round a romantic theme, as with Prokofieff's *Romeo and Juliet*.

Fin de siècle decadence in painting and literature also had its musical echoes. The interesting exhibition 'Marcel Proust and his time' which was presented at the Wildenstein

Gallery in London in 1955 recalled the faded, sometimes sickly fragrance of songs by Reynaldo Hahn and piano pieces by Gabriel Fauré.

There are parallels between different forms of contemporary artistic expression. Creative artists tend to go on ahead regardless of any communication with a public. There does not seem to be one main stream of art, but there are many currents of different styles. In an age of the scientist rather than the artist, the mathematician rather than the musician, there seems to be a preponderance of head over heart, the intellectual over the emotional. The second half of the twentieth century is an age of speed and noise, the roar of the giant airliner, the battery of the road-drill, the blare of the loud-speaker, the aural assault of the discotheque. In keeping with its time contemporary piano-writing emphasizes the instrument's percussive qualities.

As piano actions have improved in repetition and efficiency, speed of playing has increased also. To apply 'jet-propelled' tempi to the music of the past is stylistically inept. Older keyboard instruments, which belonged to eras whose tempo of life was more leisurely than ours, were not capable of excessive speed. To rattle through early music at over-fast tempi is as stylistically false as sentimentalizing the dry-eyed music composed in our time. Sir Steuart Wilson used to say that the first time he heard Hans Richter conduct the Overture of the *Marriage of Figaro* of Mozart it was at the steady pace of $\downarrow$ =120, but that thereafter every conductor he heard took it progressively faster. We have now reached a point when conductors rush Mozart willy-nilly.

Speeding in music seems to be more noticeable in English-speaking countries than in Europe. Often it covers up a lack of musicianship. Some pianists seem to be uncomfortable unless they are pushing a movement to its speed-limit. An orchestra which plays with a fine tone does not need to play too quickly. Wagner's music is given time to breathe in Germany, and so are the singers. Tchaikovsky is taken at a steady pace in Russia, played with an evenness of note-values rare to Western ears. It is not necessary for the European pianist to advertise himself as 'faster than Horowitz', which reportedly occurred in a middle-west town in North America. U.S. pianism appears to place much emphasis on speed.

Sometimes I am asked, 'What is the right tempo for this piece?' Where a composer has indicated a metronome marking there is naturally a guide to follow. But one must be sure that it is the composer's marking, and not that of an editor. There is no reason why a tempo which challenges a given metronome mark should not be adopted, provided it can be justified. Tempo is based on a speed which is suitable to the composer and his time, and one which allows comfortable articulation for the performer. There is not necessarily only one correct tempo. There may be variations between different players and yet the work can sound equally effective. Often a performance which sounds fast is due more to the vitality of the performer's style of playing, than the actual tempo. 'Allegro' can cover many shades of meaning in one composer's work. Much depends on the notation of a piece, its note-values and their disposition. Among different composers in different eras that same allegro also implies different speeds. Some of the modifications to allegro are well worth nothing—ma non troppo and maestoso. Allegro maestoso generally indicates a majestic tempo rather than a fast one.

Tempo and temperament are closely allied in music, Latin compositions being more nimble than Teutonic, Slav works more fiery than English. If you are excitable by nature then you will compose in a correspondingly lively manner. It is amusing that although no country can claim proprietary rights over a composer except his own, each regards their view of him as the right one. This is particularly noticeable in matters of tempo. A performer's temperament and his reaction under the stress of public performance also affect tempo. Some pianists play faster, others slower than they would normally. Tempo may also vary according to acoustic conditions, as very live acoustics in a hall may play havoc with too fast a tempo.

Tempo rubato (robbed time) is a vexed term, often sinned against by those who do not distinguish sufficiently between sentiment and sentimentality. Most pianists have a natural rubato; being human, they are not metronomes. Rubato can be considered as similar to the inflection of speech, a waywardness which yet falls within a strict time pattern. It is freedom, as opposed to a strict beat, and it takes its shape from the phrase itself. No sensitive pianist or sensitive speaker is going to play or speak a phrase in precise exact measures. Occasionally there is some inflection of the pace in making the rise and fall of a phrase.

We should not be aware of a performer's rubato. To be successful it must sound natural, as though proceeding from within. If it is a conscious rubato, imposed artificially from the outside, it will fail in effect and have the false ring of 'ham' acting. Even Horowitz can be unconvincing in 'applied' rubato, when he plays the second main theme of the Chopin G minor Ballade:

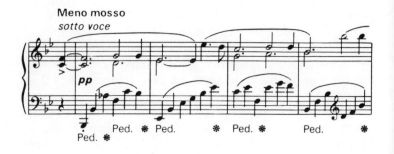

When it is employed mechanically simply because a pianist has heard that Chopin should be played with rubato, it is meaningless. Chopin kept a metronome on his piano and used it as a corrective to pupils who could not keep time. Used occasionally in this way a metronome can be of great value in showing a pianist just how much licence he is taking with the beat, and at what point.

To begin the Chopin F minor Ballade with a rubato, which one often hears, spoils the narrative style of the introduction which has a plain 'once upon a time' motive:

Andante con moto

Slight rubato is more appropriate with the rise and fall of the beautiful main theme, which is telling the story. Here the rubato is like the ebb and flow of a wave, a natural undulation rather than any conscious pulling about of the tune. If this theme is treated as a singer would phrase it, the result will be one of natural elasticity. It is only in such elastic music that rubato is appropriate.

a tempo

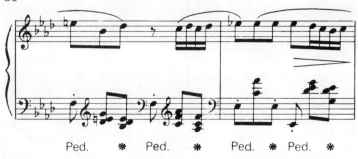

Ped.　　❋　　Ped.　　❋　　Ped.　❋　Ped.　❋

To meddle with a phrase in music of the classical period is in dubious taste, because it loses its purity of line. It does not lose its expressive quality by being played in time. An American lady once asked Schnabel whether he taught his pupils to feel the music, or to play in time. 'Madam, I teach them to feel in time.' Alfred Brendel makes Mozart's Cadenza in the first movement of his Concerto in G major K 453) sound rather self-conscious through unstylistic waywardness.

Similarly Backhaus, who usually preserved a firm line in the first movement of the Brahms B flat major Concerto, made an alarmingly out-of-context rubato which sounded quite wrong for him and the work:

Only certain romantic or post-romantic composers such as Chopin, Liszt and Rachmaninoff are suited to rubato. In Liszt's *Fantasia quasi una Sonata d'après une lecture de Dante*, Peter Katin's rigid inflexible beat destroyed the meaning of a work which needs the large gesture and elasticity even more than the B minor Sonata. Sviatoslav Richter played the second Concerto in F minor of Chopin in Moscow in 1966 with an incredible squareness of tempo which had the effect of a jet-propelled sewing-machine.

Adelina de Lara used to quote Clara Schumann as saying that rubato is out of place in Schumann's music. It is also inappropriate in certain romantic pieces where a steady clear cut relentless drive is indicated as in the so-called 'Revolutionary' Study of Chopin. It does not mean that an automaton-like effect is desirable; on the contrary, there is enough of this kind of playing at the present time.

Normally it is not practical to make a rubato until a definite tempo has been established, but if a player feels it is appropriate at the beginning of a piece, then it is justified. At the opening of the first movement of the Brahms Concerto in B flat major the horn motive is echoed by the piano. To avoid the appearance of a mechanical copy, and to give the effect of an answer to the horn, a slight inflection of the time in the last triplets of the piano quavers can be effective. It is more of a grazioso effect than a rubato.

One must be sparing in the use of rubato in a rugged composer such as Brahms. A gypsy type of melody will certainly be enhanced by it, but in the G Minor Ballade Op. 118 the relentless, stern effect is lost by any inflection of the time. Even in the lyric middle section over-applied rubato can ruin the music. A gesture in the grand manner is effective at the opening of the Grieg Piano Concerto, holding back the tempo a little in the piano's opening bar, then letting the movement flow normally. Rubato in the right hand while the left hand guides with strict time, needs to be used judiciously, in order to avoid the mannerism of playing one hand after the other so frequently indulged in by Paderewski.

CHAPTER 10

THE STYLE OF A PIECE

We don't ask the rose what trouble it has taken: we simply ask it to be a rose, and to be as different as it can from an artichoke.
Ugo Betti: *The Queen and the Rebels.*

A successful interpretation realizes a work's intrinsic nature, whether it is of epic proportions like Beethoven's *Hammerklavier Sonata* Op. 106, or a fragile miniature such as Debussy's *Flaxen-haired Girl*. But pianists of some intellectual capacity are capable of turning the rose into an artichoke, stylistically speaking, by playing a disarming Schubert Impromptu with a Lisztian brilliance which offends both the work and its composer, who was no high-powered virtuoso, but a sensitive musician who hated noise and bombast. Similarly a Chopin Study may be attacked with a hard brilliance which is foreign to the composer's style; a ballade may lose its narrative character by deviating into a nocturne in its quieter sections, the clipped rhythms of a mazurka, poised and taut, slacken into a sinuously graceful waltz. Each should be clearly recognizable in its individuality, only differentiated according to its character, as a particular kind of impromptu, study, ballade or nocturne.

Pictorial or descriptive music does not present as many problems of style as abstract music. A title is there to provide a clue. But it pre-supposes background knowledge on the part of the performer, of the place that is being described, or the painting or poem which may have inspired the work. It also relies on his imaginative powers to colour the tone to suit the atmosphere or mood of the piece. Pictorial keyboard music was not an innovation of the nineteenth

89

century piano composer. From the sixteenth century onwards harpsichord composers often gave picturesque titles to their pieces. Liszt was however the pioneer of this kind of piano music in his *Années de Pelerinage*, impressions of his travels in Switzerland and Italy as a young man.

Nineteenth century ballades, impromptus, nocturnes, mazurkas and waltzes have not developed as compositions compared with the fugues, sonatas and variations which evolved from the sixteenth and seventeenth centuries.

Fugue

The paramount consideration when playing a fugue, a form which reached its highest point in the hands of J. S. Bach, is its structure. The different voices introduce themselves in the exposition; in the middle or modulatory section they embark on a voyage of exploration into new keys, returning to the familiar harbour of the tonic in the final section. The preceding prelude sometimes has an improvisatory character, paving the way for the more important edifice to follow. If a fantasia or toccata is substituted for a prelude, the effect is more demonstrative and assertive.

Later keyboard composers have written fugues, but perhaps the majority realized that Bach had said the ultimate in this form, and either avoided it, or used it more briefly in its shortened form of fugato, as in the Liszt B minor Sonata, or in the development section of Beethoven's Sonata in A major Op. 101. When Beethoven did compose a whole fugue for the piano, in the Sonata in A flat major Op. 110, he handled it with bold freedom, breaking off in the middle to recall the earlier Aria. Similar freedom is shown in the fugue of César Franck's Prelude, Chorale and Fugue. It is interrupted by a cadenza-like passage leading to the final section, in which the Chorale is now combined with the Fugue subject. Other nineteenth century composers who wrote notably in the form include Mendelssohn and Brahms, whose Variations on a Theme by Handel are crowned by an exuberant example. In the twentieth century, Shostakovich has written 24 Preludes and Fugues

(1951). Hindemith's *Ludus Tonalis* (1942) is a collection of studies in counterpoint, tonal organization and piano playing.

Sonata

Scarlatti's 545 sonatas for harpsichord are short one-movement works in binary form, modulating to the dominant or a related key at the end of the first section. They are only sonatas in the sense of 'pieces to be sounded', sometimes with two contrasting ideas. In the eighteenth century the sonata grew into a work for several movements, one of which was in sonata or first-movement form. Like the fugue it has three sections, and can be represented by an arch.

Both Haydn and Mozart showed angularity at times in the first movements of their piano sonatas. Development sections are sometimes sketchily short, and one is often aware of the 'joins' as in unskilfully-made furniture. If the eighteenth century sonata seems to be leading up to Beethoven, nineteenth and twentieth century examples falling away from him, this is because he has written more satisfyingly, than anyone else in this medium. Whereas formal considerations appeared to dominate eighteenth century composers of sonatas, there is a fine balance of eighteenth century head and nineteenth century heart in the early and middle period Beethoven sonatas. His last five inimitable sonatas are free and expansive in construction.

As in concerto or symphony, usually the first movement of a sonata is the sturdiest, the most imposing. Care must be taken when playing a movement in sonata form to maintain its unity—first and second subjects, bridge passages, codettas and codas all bearing relationship with one another. As with the acts of a play, the movements of a sonata are related to the whole, by contrast.

Unless it is specifically indicated, as in the first movement of the Grieg Concerto in A minor, the difference between first and second subjects is better expressed by a change of mood or relaxation of tension, than by a marked ritenuto.

A sudden slowing up when the second subject is reached, weakens the movements onward pulse, as well as its line. In the Sonata in B flat minor Op. 35 Chopin has curbed the drive of the first movement by writing the second subject in semibreves, minims and crotchets, where formerly agitated quavers predominated. Any further slackening results in flaccid sentimentality. By substituting minims and crotchets for busy quavers and semiquavers, Beethoven similarly augments the note-values of the second subject of the first movement of the Sonata in C major Op. 53, but one rarely hears this played at the same tempo as the opening figure. How often does one hear a pianist 'change down' for the second subject of the first movement of the Chopin Sonata in B minor Op. 58, modulating not only into the relative major, but also into a nocturne. With its luxuriant profusion of melodic ideas, the movement is hard enough to hold together. Instead of causing it to fall to pieces when the second subject is reached, it would be better to let this theme's tempo be the standard for the whole movement. At least it would ensure a real allegro maestoso.

In a development section the character of the themes already heard is closely maintained, although the style is improvisatory. The pattern of the exposition is largely adhered to in the recapitulation, which serves as a reinforcement after the discursive development. Even the second subject is strengthened by appearing in the home key.

After Beethoven nobody seemed to equal his craftsmanship at putting a movement in sonata form together. Schubert's waywardness and 'heavenly length' do not help formal balance; sonata form tends to become diffuse in the hands of Brahms and Schumann. Liszt's loosely-knit one-movement Sonata in B minor relies for its contrast on three main sections; what unity it has is maintained by its clever thematic scheme, whereby motives are derived from others heard earlier.

Twentieth century composers do not seem to have written sonatas with much conviction. Alban Berg's fragmentary Sonata Op. 1 has a vagueness of outline which suits the spiritual discontent of its music. Arnold Bax's imposing Sonata No. 2 in G major (1919) in one movement is espisodic rather than unified. Stravinsky's sonatas for one and two pianos are cryptic and neo-classic in their harking back to the past. Like the Stravinsky works, Bartok's Sonata (1926) is in the conventional three movements. It is impelling in its ferocious strength but lies very awkwardly under the hands. Poulenc's Sonata for two pianos is typically flippant, Hindemith's four piano sonatas determinedly dry and anti-romantic. Ravel and Busoni left attractive sonatinas. Ravel's handling of his three movements is typically concise and balanced; Busoni in his Sonatina on Christ's Nativity achieves a wonderful atmosphere of holy innocence.

Variations

After tentative beginnings in the sixteenth century, keyboard variations developed through the seventeenth until the monumental achievement of the Goldberg Variations of J. S. Bach. These took their name from Karl Goldberg (1720–1770) the harpsichordist who was required to play to Count Kaiserling, Russian Ambassador at the Saxon Electoral Court at Dresden. His Excellency suffered from insomnia, and the variations were played to him one at a time, not all together as is today's practice.

C.P.E. Bach, Haydn and Mozart composed keyboard variations in the elegant *style galant* of their time, Haydn's imposing set in F minor being rococo in style, Mozart's several collections more ornamentally than musically interesting. C.P.E. Bach's Variations on La Folie d'Espagne, a much varied theme in the eighteenth and nineteenth centuries, are more boldly expressive.

As with the sonata, variation form reached its highest peak in Beethoven. Early sets, such as the 12 Variations on 'Das Waldmädchen von Wranitzky' (1796–7) and the 24 'Variations on the Arietta, Vieni, Amore von V. Righine' (1790) consist of short light variations, with extended writing only in the codas of the finales. A more legato style is evident in the middle period collections, such as those in F major Op. 34. Expansion comes with the 'Eroica' Variations (Op. 35), and virtuosity in the 32 Variations in C minor (1802). The Variations Op. 76 are a light trifle like the

Sonatas of Op. 78 and Op. 79, as though Beethoven were marking time before the intense intellectual last period, represented in this form by the superb 33 Variations on a Waltz by Diabelli.

Variation movements in the piano sonatas follow a parallel course. In the first movement of the Sonata in A flat major, Op. 26, the warm opening theme is varied lyrically and simply. After the solemn theme deep down in the bass, the variations in the central movement of the *Appassionata Sonata,* Op. 57 gradually rise into the upper registers of the piano, note-values decreasing successively during their progress to the thinner treble strings. Up till now variations adhere closely to the theme's metrical and harmonic design, but in the last sonatas Beethoven's variation technique is transformed and becomes more creative. The masterful handling of the variations in the second movement of the Sonata in C minor, Op. 111 assures the work of its final apotheosis. Here again there is an ascent to the upper strata of the piano which adds to the concluding sublimity.

Philosophy has no part in Variations by Brahms, who displays tremendous technical skill in handling devices of the musician's craft in his Variations on an Original Theme Op. 26. In the virtuoso sets of Op. 24 and Op. 35 (on Handel and Paganini themes) the pianist faces some of the greatest technical challenges in his repertoire. Variations were a keyboard favourite form of other nineteenth century composers, no doubt because of their possibilities for spectacular breadth, but they rarely appear in twentieth century piano writing. Anton Webern's Variations, Op. 26 for piano are enigmatic, spare and compressed.

The strict classical attitude to tempo in variation form, which advocates the same speed throughout, unless the composer indicates to the contrary, leads to rigidity of expression from Beethoven onwards. It is more a matter of tempo relationship between the variations and the theme, rather than a mechanical sameness.

Dance forms.

Dance forms, which date back to the beginning of keyboard

music, do not pose many problems of style once a pianist distinguishes clearly the character and tempi of different dances—graciously flowing allemande, nimble-footed bourrée, supple courante or lively gigue. The suites which were strung together from them, have a monotony of key that keeps interest focussed on the slow or quick nature of the dances.

Other forms

There are many small fanciful nineteenth century pieces whose charm belies the impersonality of their titles—the delicate flourish of an arabesque, short narrative of a novelette, or the impromptu, which should sound as though improvised on the spot. The most spontaneous of the Chopin Impromptus is that in F sharp major, Op. 36. Its four sections are strongly contrasted. The first meanders uncertainly, abruptly interrupted by a purposeful march, as taut as the opening section is elastic. Tension is relaxed on the return of the theme, now a semitone lower in F major, embroidered by triplets of quavers. Finally a warm left-hand cello melody is accompanied by swift demisemiquavers in the right hand. A short epilogue of musing quaver chords and the brilliant improvization is over. Other Chopin Impromptus are harder to realize, owing to their set ternary form, the repetition of the third section destroying the improvisatory effect. If an impromptu is too strictly composed, spontaneity is difficult to achieve. Occasionally the Schubert Impromptus have this disadvantage. Gabriel Fauré sometimes avoided a cut-and-dried effect by repeating the episode as well as the main section.

Brahms gave the rather colourless title of Intermezzo to many of his piano pieces. They are widely variable mood-pictures from grave melancholy (Op. 118, No. 6 in E flat minor) to easy gaiety (C major, Op. 119). The more extravagantly emotional Rhapsody found a champion in Liszt, whose flamboyance revelled in this form, so suitable in its freedom for the sentiments expressed in high-flown Hungarian gypsy songs. Dohnanyi's Rhapsodies do not have quite the same abandon. Brahm's sturdy Rhapsody in E flat major Op. 119 concludes, in the regret of his last years, in the minor key. Another free form, the fantasia, has been neither fixed nor evolutionary since its inception in the early days of keyboard music, but of course it reflects the style and times of its composers.

In the nineteenth century the prelude developed a new connotation. From being an introductory or supporting— piece before a fugue or suite, it developed an independent status of its own. No later composer has emulated the miniature perfection of Chopin's 24 Preludes, most romantic of his compositions. In a few bars he created a striking sense of atmosphere, as deftly as Chekov in a few lines of prose. Chopin's collection was imitated by Scriabine, Rachmaninov and Shostakovich. Rachmaninov, particularly, enlarged its form. Debussy went a step further by giving his series extra-musical visual or literary associations with scenes of natural beauty—the *Submerged Cathedral*, *Fireworks*, *Heather* etc.

Studies of Clementi, Cramer and Czerny, intended for private finger-drill, opened up the pianist's technical possibilities in the early nineteenth century. Chopin, Schumann and Liszt brought the study into the concert-hall, Chopin raising it to a work of art as well as of technique. Schumann's *Etudes Symphoniques* which are intricate and involved, take on a wider aspect than their formidable technical purpose, by being cast in the form of variations. Liszt often gave his concert studies extraneous emotional or musical significance by attaching to them titles such as *Forest Murmurs*, *Snow-Plough*, *Remembrance*, or *A Sigh*. Rachmaninov's *Etudes—Tableaux* have unstated pictorial associations. As might be expected, Debussy in his 12 *Etudes* was as interested in exploring possibilities of tone-colour as in technical problems. Other notable writers of concert studies such as Saint-Saëns and Dohnanyi, do not disguise their technical purpose, but have left stimulating examples none the less.

Unlike a painting, which is usually secure from the hands of vandals, a musical work is at the mercy of an arranger after its composer has been dead for fifty years. It may then be defaced or cheapened in any way. Accordingly melodies of Chopin, Tchaikovsky, Liszt and many others have been besmirched with tawdry sentimental words, and vulgarized with 'pop' rhythms. J. S. Bach has been given 'the full treatment' by the pop world in electronic or 'switched-on' Bach, Bach goes to Town, or in vocalized fugues. Although when Bach's music is played on modern instruments it amounts to arrangement, it is not the debasement which occurs here. Sometimes a complete classical work is given a 'new look'. For instance one of the most beautiful of operas, *Carmen*, was hardly improved in its new version of Carmen Jones. *The Song of Norway* cheapened Grieg and his music, to suit the popular sentimentality of the 'musical'.

To arrange from one medium to another is one thing; but to jazz up something beautiful in itself only mirrors the mentality of those who perpetrate these acts, and the far larger numbers who condone them.

Part II

CHAPTER 1

J.S. Bach on the Modern Piano

It is a depressing experience to play a piece by Bach on the clavichord or harpsichord, and then on the piano. The gulf between the two types of instrument is immediately apparent. Bach never composed for the pianoforte, which was in its infancy during his lifetime, and apparently never liked it. After trying pianos of Gottfried Silbermann in 1736 he complained of their heaviness of touch. What would he think of the 49 grammes weight of today's piano key? Heaviness cannot have been the only cause of his dissatisfaction. Although better pleased with other Silbermann pianos he examined in 1747, the type of sound produced by the new pianoforte was so different, that he would never have composed contrapuntal music for it. Horizontally flowing voices of a fugue are far more appropriate to the clarity and evenly-distributed tone of clavichord or harpsichord.

It is most unfortunate that the bulk of Bach's clavier music was not published until the beginning of the nineteenth century, when the harpsichord and clavichord had already been superseded by the pianoforte. Although the early nineteenth century piano was more suited to Bach's music than our piano, it was foreign to its style. The transference of Bach's clavier music to the piano is almost as much a transcription as any organ arrangement. In many respects the transcription of an organ work can be more faithfully realized on the piano than a clavier composition because the piano's sonority has more in common with the organ than with the harpsichord.

Although it imposed a false style on Bach's clavier music, nevertheless the new school of pianism welcomed it enthusiastically. Carl Czerny referred to Bach as the teacher and lawgiver to all future time. 'Sebastian Bach still stands a gigantic image before us, rather wondered at than understood'. Before he gave a piano recital Chopin would retire for several weeks with the 48 Preludes and Fugues, knowing what excellent discipline they were for the fingers. At the end of the century Busoni propounded that 'Bach is the foundation of piano-playing, Liszt the summit. The two make Beethoven possible'.

The virtual disappearance of the clavichord and harpsichord in the nineteenth century resulted in a break in the tradition of the playing of these instruments. The false style imposed on the clavier music was so forceful that even the modern harpsichordist is likely to approach it with the nineteenth century in mind. In spite of the efforts of musicologists in the twentieth century the harpsichordist is often uncertain in his interpretation of Bach. The pianist may be bewildered.

The earliest editions of the Well-Tempered Clavier appeared in 1801, 50 years after Bach's death, from Nägeli in Zürich, Simrock in Bonn, Hoffmeister in Vienna, and Hoffmeister and Kühnel in Leipzig. They were taken from rare surviving Bach autographs or from copies by pupils, and were refreshingly free from additions of any kind. Most succeeding editions have been littered with indications of tempo, dynamics and phrasing. Editors such as Czerny, Bischoff, Busoni, Klindworth, Teichmüller and Bartok were unable to leave the text alone. The Bachgesellschaft edition not only gave a text refreshingly free from the usual superfluous markings, but also listed its sources. Tovey was content to give his instructions in the form of a commentary, merely suggesting marks of tempo.

To get some idea of the many different editorial approaches to Bach's music on the piano, we can examine one Prelude and Fugue No. 2 in C minor (Bk. I, Well-Tempered Clavier). Kroll for Peters, the Bach-Gesellschaft and the Henle Verlag, like the pioneers of 1801, leave everything to the player, only indicating Bach's marks of presto (Bar 28) adagio (bar 34) and allegro (bar 35) in the prelude. Czerny (Vienna 1838) who was preparing his edition for piano students not only indicated 'the proper marks of expression' (which Bach had omitted to do) but 'the exact time of each movement'. In the Prelude these were forte for the greater part, with some piano bars to give contrast. Bar 28 (presto) he marks fortissimo; and there is an effective drop to *pp* at the adagio (bar 34).

Busoni also recommends an energetic approach, even describing the Prelude as a 'river of flames' a typical nineteenth century virtuoso approach. The adagio he marks 'recitando, drammatico', Bischoff marks the Prelude 'energico'. Bartok advocates a forte alternating with mezzo-forte. Harold Brooke for Novello, veers between forte and fortissimo throughout. Tovey, on the other hand, takes a quiet clavichord view of this prelude.

Most editors favour a quiet scheme of dynamics in the fugue, building up to bolder proportions in the final section, where both Czerny and Busoni double the bass with its lower octave in bar 26. This imitation of the harpsichord's 16 foot stop does not sound natural on the piano.

In matters of tempo there is much variation between editors. Czerny begins the Prelude Allegro Vivace ($\quarternote = 144$) a quick speed which leaves little room for contrast when Bach's presto is reached at Bar 28. In bar 36 he adds a rallentando, a lento at bar 37, and a ritenuto in bar 38. Fritz Rothschild in his *Handbook* to the performance of the forty eight Preludes and Fugues according to the rules of the old tradition gives a metronome marking of $\quarternote = 60$, a snail's pace which suggests a slow-practice tempo. It is in accordance with his theory that tempo can be gauged from the time-signatures and note-values of each Prelude and Fugue. This pedestrian speed is applied by Helmut Walcha in his harpsichord recording of the Well-Tempered Clavier for Deutsche Gramophon Gesellschaft. It sounds pedantic. Busoni naturally takes a quick virtuoso view of the Prelude Allegro con fuoco. Tovey suggests something between these two extremes, pointing out that a very quick tempo would be the merest buzz of sound on a clavichord. A tempo of ♩=80 seems to be more appropriate when this Prelude is played on the piano, than those of Czerny, Busoni or Rothschild. Common sense and musicality are better arbiters of style than hidebound theory or the art of finger-dexterity.

Most editors agree that the fugue is a graciously-flowing dance movement, and recommend a moderate speed. Czerny indicates Allegretto moderato (♩=80) Busoni Allegretto vivacemente, Bischoff Grazioso.

Many different suggestions are made as to the touch and phrasing of this Prelude and Fugue. Rothschild indicates non-legato for both. Czerny and Busoni take a legato view of the Prelude. Busoni's edition of the Well-Tempered Clavier provides the pianist with a comprehensive manual of piano technique in the foot-notes. From this C minor Prelude he evolves virtuoso studies in octaves, thirds and sixths, and another useful exercise in which the little finger is held as a minim. Bartok accents the first and third beats, and has a crescendo and diminuendo from the first to the second beats, and from the third to the fourth similarly.

In the Fugue Czerny marks the subject staccato throughout; Brooke keeps it completely legato, Busoni and Bartok break it up into a mixture of legato and staccato

Busoni

Bartok

while Bischoff makes it legato, but breaks up the phrasing:

Bischoff

Somebody else might phrase it:

From all these treatments of one of the shortest of the Preludes and Fugues it can be seen what has happened to Bach's original manuscripts. For the musician the most satisfying edition is the plain unadorned text, with its source and any variants, named. The player then makes his own edition, using his own phrasing and dynamics. There are many different views of Bach on clavichord, harpsichord and pianoforte, and each player believes his is the right one. 'You play him your way, dear, and I will continue to play him his way' was Wanda Landowska's confident assertion to a pianist colleague. On being asked whose edition of the *Chromatic Fantasia and Fugue* he used, Edwin Fischer's reply was, 'My own, of course.'

The well-tempered Clavier does not specify whether Bach had clavichord or harpsichord in mind. Certainly it was not the pianoforte. Some writers have concluded that the first book was composed for the clavichord, the second for harpsichord. The first book (1722), which has always been the more popular, has a clavichord intimacy in many of its members. No. 1 in C major is most expressive on the delicately-shaded clavichord. No. 5 in D major needs a harpsichord for its trenchant brilliancy to be fully realized. No. 4 in C Sharp minor has a cantabile Prelude and a Fugue whose organ-like breadth is better served by the piano than either of the earlier instruments, although its part-writing is more clearly revealed on these.

In Book II (1744) a bold fugue such as No. 20 in A minor, or a brilliant Prelude like No. 5 in D major need a harpsichord to do them full justice. No. 9 in E major suggests the organ in both Prelude and Fugue. Elsewhere the range is broader than in the first book. Some (Nos. 16 and 17) need an orchestra rather than a keyboard instrument.

But a delicate Prelude like No. 3 sounds better on a clavichord.

Bach suffered a good deal at the hands of nineteenth century appreciative 'restorers' who did not hesitate to amplify passages or change notes if they wished. Hans von Bülow prepared a piano edition of the Chromatic Fantasia and Fugue which is tantamount to a transcription. Characteristically it was praised by Busoni as being a suitable modern version. Often it seems as much von Bülow as Bach with its doublings of single notes into sixths or eighths.

Yet in a large hall, stylistic anchronisms notwithstanding, a good transcription of an organ work is probably more satisfactory to piano, pianist and audience than the presentation of original clavichord or harpsichord pieces. Stylistically a small hall and a smaller grand may be more successful with the latter.

Two mediums of voice and instrument are fused in Bach's organ chorale-preludes, which are among his most moving keyboard compositions. In piano arrangement they are naturally at second-best, but they lend themselves more to arrangement than the bigger organ works, owing to their singing quality and smaller size. Busoni's fine transcriptions of several of them were prefaced with the astounding remark that they should be played 'without feeling'. They are among Bach's most emotional works; and Busoni was probably aiming at the avoidance of sentimentality. In the period between the two World Wars it became fashionable for pianists to arrange Bach chorale-preludes for one or two pianos. Not all of these arrangements were in good taste; some seem to be more suited to a tea-shop than to a concert hall.

SOME PROBLEMS IN THE PERFORMANCE OF J. S. BACH ON THE PIANO

Pedalling

To forbid the use of the piano's sustaining pedal in Bach's music is to be ignorant of the sound of the clavichord and harpsichord. There is a natural sustaining of sound on the latter instrument which the piano lacks. It would be foolish to smudge a fast movement by the use of the pedal, but it can be a tactful adjunct to the hands in helping them over an awkward join or in a slow movement where a melody needs support. Bolder pedalling can be applied in the organ transcriptions, where more resonance is desirable. The middle pedal can be used as a substitute for the organist's foot, in sustaining a long pedal note.

Touch

In imitation of a crisp harpsichord effect, non-legato or a finger staccato touch in a quick movement is appropriate. The Prelude to the English Suite in A minor responds well to a mixture of non-legato and legato, while the Prelude in D major (Book I, *Well-Tempered Clavier*) is eminently suited to a detached finger touch. Obviously in a slow singing movement non-legato is out of place. Where string tone is suggested, as in the B flat minor Prelude (Book 1, No. 22, W.T.C.). the utmost legato can be aimed at. Some quiet pieces are more successful on the piano than on the harpsichord. Bach's Clavier arrangement of the slow movement from an oboe concerto ascribed to Marcello, is far more effective on the piano, because of the nature of the original— oboe with string accompaniment. A better tonal balance between melody and accompaniment is possible on the piano. Also the melody itself can be more expressively shaped.

Rothschild's listing of legato and non-legato for each Prelude and Fugue of the Forty-eight is a tiresome enumeration which few players could regard with patience. Occasionally his indications of non-legato seem misplaced, as in the cantando Prelude in G sharp minor (No. 18, Bk. 1, W.T.C.). Where a work is suited to the clavichord, legato is appropriate on the piano; a bolder harpsichord type of piece needs non-legato to express its brilliance.

Ornamentation

This is the thorniest of all problems in playing Bach on the piano, as what suits the timbre of the harpsichord does not necessarily fit the piano's thicker sound. Bach left us a guide to his ornaments in the Explication he made for Wilhelm Friedman Bach's instruction in 1720. Other decorative conventions of the eighteenth century have also been lost with the virtual disappearance of the harpsichord in the nineteenth century. What the eighteenth century harpsi-chordist would have known instinctively, we can only guess at. Should a trill always begin on the upper note? The opening figure of the Concerto for 2 Claviers in C major sounds rather forced and pedantic when the trill begins on the upper note, particularly when the theme is rising by step from E to F. On the other hand by beginning on the upper note, a triplet at the end of the trill is avoided. The number of repercussions of a trill will naturally depend on the context. A slow trill is suitable to a gravely melodic chorale-prelude such as '*O mensch, bewein dein Sünde gross*' (O Man, thy grievous sin bemoan), but over a long note a rapid trill is appropriate (G minor Prelude No. 16, Bk. 1 W.T.C.).

The trill at the opening of the B flat major Partita presents a particular problem for the pianist. On the harpsichord a long trill beginning on the upper note is possible because of its feather-weight touch; on the piano it seems too fussy. A simple turn beginning on the principal note has a more graceful effect. Pianists sometimes forget that ornamentation is graceful embellishment which decorates the music. It suits the harpsichord, fortepiano and early nineteenth century piano far more than the modern piano. Imitation of a singer's deft and light ornamentation becomes a pianist.

Sometimes ornaments can be added at the player's will, but care must be exercised. The ornamental variant of the fourth Prelude in C sharp minor (Bk. 1, W.T.C.) sounds out of place on the piano; even on the harpsichord it sounds over-elaborate, spoiling the piece's simple lyricism.

Double-dotting

Where double-dotting is possible, as in the subject of the D. major Fugue (No. V, Bk. 1, W.T.C.) the ♩. ♪ figure,

which sounds very effective on the harpsichord as ♩.. ♪ on
the heavier piano sounds more effective as written. Here
again experts differ—Helmut Walcha in his harpsichord
recording does not double-dot this fugue at all. Tovey
recommends double-dotting of the principal subject, but
not of the smoother episode in the middle section. Rothschild advocates double-dotting throughout. Who is right?

The concerted works

In these the harpsichord is much more effective than the
piano, which overweights the strings. Bernard Shaw in a
letter to Harriet Cohen (8 February 1928) complains of the
use of a piano in the Brandenburg Concerto No. 5 for Flute,
Violin, Clavier and strings. 'The first thing that you have to
grasp is that the modern steel grand pianoforte is so plainly
inferior in tone to violin and flute (for instance) that it
should never be brought into immediate rivalry with them.
No artifice of touch that you can possibly employ can give
you a dog's chance when, in Bach, you have to follow a
solo flute and solo violin in a single-line melody on the
piano. You cannot disguise the atrocious inferiority of the
tone. You must play on the harpsichord, where the tone is
so completely different that it never sounds like a bad imitation of the flute'.

Where there is no question of balance or contrast with
other instruments a piano may be acceptable, as in a solo
recital, but in the clavier concertos the Baroque flavour is
lost in the leaden weight of the piano's tone.

Bach pianists in the twentieth century

In the twentieth century there have been many distinguished
Bach pianists, who have shown the influence of the current
thought on Bach of their time. Edwin Fischer brought warm
humanity to Bach's music, playing with all the tonal beauty
possible on the piano. He never allowed the 'line' of the
music to be obscured, but kept a balance between outline
and content, architectural shape and feeling.

The English school of Bach pianists has tended to see him

as a gentle clavichordist, a view no doubt influenced by Tovey. Evelyn Howard-Jones brought a distinguished sense of style to the Well-Tempered Clavier, and Harold Samuel, another Bach specialist, collaborated with Tovey in providing fingering for his edition of the forty-eight Preludes and Fugues. It has often been criticized as unpractical. Harriet Cohen used distinctive piano colour in her Bach playing, even pastel shades, but never allowed the music to lose its line.

Bach harpsichord playing in the twentieth Century

There seem to be as many different views of Bach on the harpsichord as there are on the piano. Some harpsichordists deny him a 16 foot stop, as there is doubt as to whether it was available on the harpsichord of his time. Wanda Landowska took a virtuoso view of Bach on her powerful Pleyel instrument, which resembled an organ. The vitality of her playing was compelling.

Other harpsichordists play in an intellectual style which sometimes becomes monotonous. In the interests of 'purity' they adopt one scheme of registration throughout a Prelude and Fugue.

Thurston Dart in *The Interpretation of Music* (Hutchinson 1954) says that instruments should not borrow one another's characteristics. From a musical point of view this is rather a severe argument. If the harpsichordist wants to imitate the clavichord in a Prelude and Fugue which is obviously suited to it, no stylistic harm is done. Nor does colourful registration in the style of an organ, detract from a work.

SOME POINTS OF INTERPRETATION

Line

Line is supremely important in Bach's music. This can be maintained by strict observance of the time, with inflections where suitable—to make a dramatic point in a fugue, as for example in the C minor Fugue of Book 1 at the cadential close before the coda (bar). A compulsory ritardando at the end of every fugue becomes a mannerism. It is a matter for the player's judgment, more apt at the end of a broadly-flowing than of a nimble fugue.

Rhythmic buoyancy is very important to the tautness of a lively fugue. Many of Bach's fugues are dance movements, when each note of the subject should bounce with elation. It was rhythmic *élan* which made Landowska's playing so memorable.

Tempo

Tempo ought to be related to clavichord or harpsichord in a stylistic performance. The eighteenth century was not an age of jet-propulsion, and to rattle off Bach's music on the piano reflects a pianist's shallow appreciation of it. Transcriptions of organ works can be taken a little faster than at an organ speed if necessary, as the piano lacks the organ's sustaining power, but one can only deplore a performance of the closing fugue of the Bach-Busoni Toccata in C major, which starts off at a gallop but has to pull up when the writing becomes more difficult.

Dynamics

Albert Schweitzer suggests a dynamic in accordance with the structure of a fugue. He cites as an example the D major Fugue of Book 1 (W.T.C.) For the exposition and final section he suggests forte, for the middle section piano. On the piano this does not exclude variations within those sections, otherwise the effect would be wooden if kept uniformly loud or soft. A black and white pattern cannot apply to all fugues however. Some gradually build up from a quiet beginning to a tremendous climax, as in the Fugue following the Chromatic Fantasia. Blocks of tone can also be effective in the Prelude to the English Suite in A minor. It responds to forte until bar 55, when the subsidiary theme can drop down to *pp, mf* or *f* in references to the principal subject, and forte when the opening section returns.

It is evident that there are many different ways of playing Bach, and he is a brave person who can claim, like Landowska to play him 'his way'. His greatness as a composer allows for these variations, but complication has been added by the instrusion of the pianoforte, and the loss of harpsichord traditions of playing.

Bach's music is only for the real music-lover. It is not for those who want superficial glitter or a facile emotional response. In it are to be found the deepest of feelings, consummate mastery of formal procedures, counterpoint, harmony and melody, balanced by an equally masterful keyboard technique. Bach demands a sound intellectual approach. But his music requires more than intelligence for its realizations. It needs human warmth, character and integrity.

CHAPTER 2

EARLY PIANO COMPOSITION IN THE EIGHTEENTH CENTURY

Although the pianoforte was invented in 1709, it was not until the 1770s that composers began to write exclusively for it at the expense of the clavichord and harpsichord. Keyboard instruments of the 1970s bear little relationship in sound and touch to those of 1870, still less to those of 1770. In the first half of the eighteenth century composers still thought in terms of harpsichord and clavichord. None of the three great keyboard figures born in 1685, J. S. Bach, Händel or D. Scarlatti wrote for an instrument which was still more or less of a curiosity when they died. Composers with the life-span of George Christoph Wagenseil (1715–77) and Thomas Arne (1710–78) must have favoured earlier instruments too.

The eldest of Bach's sons, Carl Philip Emmanuel, appears to have retained a preference for the clavichord, although he did write for the piano in 1752. Later he composed a double concerto for harpsichord and fortepiano. The model by Fritz (1751) in the Victoria and Albert Museum shows that the mid-eighteenth century German clavichord could reach almost the size of a square piano, which must have increased its volume and powers of expression, yet C.P.E. Bach's compositions sometimes seem more appropriate to the harpsichord than to either clavichord or pianoforte e.g. his variations on *La Folie d'Espagne*.

In his search for a different style of writing from his father's, monophonic as opposed to polyphonic, C.P.E.

113

Bach's keyboard music sometimes seems a little unformed and awkward. In common with many other eighteenth century composers he also suffered from the limitation of having to compose many of his works for particular individuals, wealthy patrons or gifted pupils, and he did not feel that these works had the same value as the few he wrote freely for his own use. He even seemed to resent having to write to suit the tastes of 'the public'. His chief interest in later years lay in writing for the fortepiano, so that 'playing should resemble singing as much as possible, in spite of the deficiency in the piano's sustaining power'.

His sixty-five sonatas mark an intermediate stage in the transition from old to modern sonata form. They are not wanting in development of ideas, although the development section of a movement often consists of a repetition of the exposition in the dominant. At the end of a first movement there might be a fermata or pause, when the player was expected to provide an improvised cadenza, a practice which did not continue for long, and had been dropped by the 1770s. Both Haydn and Mozart acknowledged their debt to C.P.E. Bach's Sonatas, and it is a pity that they are not as easily available in publication to the piano student, as those of the later composers who overshadowed him.

Similar obscurity surrounds Johann Christian Bach's thirty-five piano sonatas. Known as the 'London' Bach because of his residence there from 1763, he might be more aptly named the Italian Bach. He was the one member of the family who forsook the Protestant faith and went over to Rome, his style being greatly influenced by his student days in Italy with Padre Martini and his love of Italian opera. This may explain why Mozart was so sympathetic towards his composition, and lamented his death in 1782. His sonatas occasionally show affinity with Mozart's, particularly the Sonata in C minor Op. 17, No. 2. His style seems less expansive and expressive than that of Carl Philip Emmanuel, with whom he studied composition in Berlin after the death of his father. Formally the two have much in common, although Johann Christian avoided the device of a fermata at the end of a first movement. Development sections, like those of his brother, tend to be repetitive, not an extension of material already heard. Thematically the sonatas are not always interesting, and the texture of the music in its two parts, tends to become monotonous. Johann Christian however was the only one of Bach's sons who championed the new pianoforte to the exclusion of clavichord and harpsichord.

These early sonatas by Bach's sons have been overshadowed by those of Haydn and Mozart, which have more vivacity and lightness. But it would be useful in enabling us to get the whole period in stylistic perspective if players would make more excursion into unfamiliar eighteenth century sonatas. It is a field waiting to be explored by gramophone companies, preferably on a modern prototype of eighteenth century fortepiano, not on the big, booming, contemporary piano.

Franz Josef Haydn (1732–1809) began by composing for the harpsichord but changed over to fortepiano in mid-career. Christa Landon in the excellent Universal edition of Haydn Sonatas deduces this from the specifically pianoforte marks of expression which appear from No. 20 (Hoboken index) onwards (1771). Sforzando (*sf*) and fortepiano (*fp*) are markings inapplicable to harpsichord music. Before, the sonatas had been called Divertimenti. Haydn's change-over to the fortepiano was no doubt influenced by the excellence of the Viennese instruments of Anton Walter, Späth, Streicher and Stein. The light Viennese action made for an easy touch and brilliant execution. Although Haydn was never an accomplished virtuoso as was Mozart, who was familiar with the new fortepiano at an early age, his later sonatas show a remarkable development in keyboard technique no doubt influenced by those of Clementi and Mozart.

As in the case of the 104 Symphonies, comparatively few of Haydn's sixty Sonatas are heard in public, although Sviatoslav Richter and Malcolm Frager are two pianists who have revived several unfamiliar ones. The most frequently played is the last in E flat major (Hoboken No. 52) often called misleadingly No. 1, and dated 1794. The martial chords of the opening movement would not be idiomatic on the harpsichord. The florid demisemiquaver passage work, the expressive melody of the slow movement would also be difficult to realize on the harpsichord. This sonata has some bold changes of key. At the beginning of the development section of the first movement there is an abrupt transition from B flat major to G major, through a chromatic rise by semitones in the melody. Instead of proceeding to C major however, the second subject is unexpectedly heard in E major. This same key is used for the slow movement, unusual in a Sonata whose outer movements are in E flat. Fifty years after the first sonatas of C.P.E. Bach, one can here see a great expansion in the development section of this first movement. Now it has freedom and independence, not mere repetition. This sonata has a breadth of conception more symphonic than pianistic. The theme of the last movement is repeated a semitone higher, surprise tactics which anticipate Beethoven's opening theme of the Appassionata Sonata.

Vladimir Horowitz, who popularized this Sonata in a brilliant 78 r.p.m. recording of the 1930s, shows a lamentable lapse of taste in his post-war L.P. version in which excessive speed ruins the music; twentieth century jet-propulsion is fatal to Haydn.

Other late Haydn sonatas are more interesting to the pianist than their predecessors. The F minor Variations of 1793 (un poco divertimento) also show his later technical freedom, particularly in the coda, where a dramatic outburst takes the work out of the formal rococo frame of the preceding variations.

The Viennese School invested the sonata with a pleasing melodic quality, a spontaneity and a rhythmic sprightliness which had been lacking in the examples of Bach's sons. These high spirits however, are difficult to maintain on the contemporary grand piano, whose massiveness and solidity conflict with their nature. The contemporary pianist cannot help adjusting a Haydn Sonata to suit his piano; it is impossible to make the piano fit the work.

Muzio Clementi (1752–1832), born twenty years later than Haydn, had more influence on his contemporaries than the neglect of his sixty-four sonatas would imply today. His protagonists, in drawing attention to their merit, make extravagant claims by attributing to him a new piano style 'at one stroke', or by crediting the difference between Mozart's last Sonata (K576) and Beethoven's first, to him alone. This is an oversimplification which becomes obvious when a similar comparison is made between Mozart's last and Beethoven's first symphony. Clementi's sonatas have a pianistic quality which is a joy to the player. Like the set of studies *Gradus ad Parnassum*, they lie perfectly under the hand. Undoubtedly Clementi's virtuosity had a great influence on the writing of Haydn, Mozart and Beethoven, but to suggest that he changed piano style overnight by the composition of his sonatas in 1773, is surely going too far. There are inter-acting stylistic influences within a given period, but there is also an overall period style.

Clementi's main contribution to keyboard writing was his technical ability, his skill in writing double thirds, broken octaves. The expansive breadth of his sonatas brought new freedom, a new atmosphere to the sonata. Not only was Clementi a champion of the new instrument ('father of the pianoforte' as his epitaph in Westminster Abbey calls him) but in an age of versatile musicians he combined an extra-ordinary number of talents—composer, virtuoso, editor of eighteenth century music, publisher and piano-maker. If the piano recitalist wishes to stick to the letter of his occupation then he need in his programme-building go back no further than Clementi, Haydn, Mozart, C.P.E. and J. C. Bach.

Mozart's piano writing suffers most of all when transferred to the modern grand. It distorts his music and the pianist who plays a Mozart concerto is faced with a dilemma for which there is no solution. Either he must refine the music, caress his instrument to produce an effect so rounded that it could never belong to Mozart, or he must magnify it so that it loses its sensitivity. Other problems arise too over the size of orchestral string forces, piano cadenzas and embellish-ment. Where Mozart left no cadenzas, the performer may play his own or use someone else's. He may run into stylistic trouble if its author is romantically inclined, when the effect tends to be amusing. The problems of embellishment are equally formidable. How to fill out bars in which Mozart may have left only an outline of the harmony?

What to do at a fermata or 'eingang' into another section? A pianist's taste and judgment are the only guide here.

On the modern piano an over-decorated slow movement such as that of the A major concerto (K488) may sound fussy and out of place. With the contemporary piano's thick tone, plain unembellished playing of the notes may be more satisfactory. Bearing in mind the size of the modern orchestral string bass section, it seems unnecessary for the pianist to supply any additional bass in the orchestral tuttis, as was apparently the original custom.

Though it is an anachronism for him to be playing this music on an iron-framed concert grand at all, the pianist on his own in a Mozart Sonata is more fortunate. Faced with the dramatic first movements of the Sonatas in C minor (K457) or A minor (K310) he will have to capitulate to the modern piano to a certain extent by inflating the music if he is not to emasculate its virility. A purely singing piece such as the Adagio in B minor (K540) can be made acceptable on the modern piano by meticulous tonal control. Paderewski achieved a miracle of timelessness in his recording of the Rondo in A minor (K511) although his mellow performance is assisted by a pre-1939 piano. Light-fingered movements such as the outer ones of the Sonata in D (K576) may imitate the spiky clarity of a fortepiano by a non-legato touch concentrating on finger and wrist.

Mozart's music does not suit the harpsichord, so embedded in his keyboard style in the fortepiano. His compositions remain the modern pianist's biggest challenge, because of their inevitable transference to an unnatural medium whose heaviness impedes their decorative quality.

CHAPTER 3

BEETHOVEN—THE THREE STYLES

The year of Beethoven's birth, 1770, was the beginning of the decade when keyboard composers rejected clavichord and harpsichord. Henceforth there was no uncertainty or ambiguity about keyboard writing. Although his sonatas were to be published for many years as suitable for harpsichord or pianoforte, Beethoven's very first sonata is unthinkable on the harpsichord, so unmistakeably pianistic is it. Whereas Haydn and Mozart regarded performance on harpsichord and pianoforte as interchangeable in their youth, Beethoven in his formative years thought of the keyboard solely in terms of the piano.

When Beethoven came to write his first sonatas, sonata-form was already well-developed. Its ground-plan was established, following the gropings of Bach's sons, the freer style adopted by Muzio Clementi, and the last sonatas of Haydn and Mozart, miniature symphonies for the piano. Beethoven wrote best in large forms, and sonata form was the ideal framework for his musical thinking. He transformed it with a life it had never before possessed, impressed on it a logic which it has never since regained.

To account for the difference between the last pianoforte sonata of Mozart and the first of Beethoven (a space of seven years), it is not enough to give all the credit to Clementi as does C. M. Girdlestone (*Music and Letters*, Vol. XIII). The fundamental difference is in the character of the men themselves. Mozart and Haydn also, had been influenced by

Clementi, although Mozart was very sarcastic about his pianistic ability. The forceful stamp of Beethoven's personality is already evident in the mixture of various musical ideas that we find in his first piano sonatas.

Surely there has never been a more angry young composer than Beethoven; particularly in the tension which is reflected in his early works, although he retained an irascibility induced by ill-health all his life. Never regarding the piano as a harpsichord with hammers, he had a more individualistic piano style than his predecessors, more legato and depth of tone. His touch was of a more weighty German penetration than the elegance of his Austrian predecessors.

The piano began its process of expansion in Beethoven's lifetime but it was still a smaller instrument with a correspondingly smaller sound than ours, although weaker string tension gave it a purer sound. It was consequently more suited to Beethoven's conciseness of thought. On the Broadwood pianos of his day it was also possible to proceed gradually from one to three strings and vice versa, thus giving a crescendo or diminuendo in addition to that supplied by the hands. Economy in the use of the sustaining pedal is a stylistic help on our piano, with its greater strength.

Beethoven appreciated the deeper English or German action in contrast with the shallow Viennese instruments. In the urgency of what he wanted to say, Beethoven was not looking for a suavely elegant piano, his vigorous nature was more interested in matter than manner, in an instrument which encouraged sustained legato playing, not an airy non-legato, in one capable of resisting thrust from the whole arm, not merely from the wrist and fore-arm. Beethoven still continued the use of *fp* (fortepiano) as a mark of expression as used by Haydn and Mozart. This special effect, which involves a sudden partial releasing of tone on a note or chord, is more suited to a piano with a light action and tone. It is difficult to manage on our piano, but most effective when it can be done. Modern composers generally avoid it, although Michael Tippett has revived the *fp* in his Sonata No. 2 (1962) and called it a 'diamond note'.

It is often said that Beethoven would have appreciated the

size and power of the contemporary piano. No doubt his poor hearing would have benefited from it, but it is difficult to correlate the characteristics of the modern piano with Beethoven's pantheistic thinking. To him any piano would be limited. The contemporary piano whilst broadening the volume of the early nineteenth century piano by its higher string tension blunts the cutting edge of its tone.

Certain of the sonatas and piano concertos have been vulgarized by the addition of names bestowed on them by publishers or critics although these names have secured for some sonatas a popularity over their fellows. Nevertheless names are entirely unnecessary in works of absolute music, and are best avoided as meaningless.

Wilhelm von Lenz in his *Beethoven and his Three Styles* divides the sonatas into three periods, beginning the second with the Sonatas of Opus 31, when Beethoven said that he was taking a new path, and the third with the Sonata in A major, Op. 101. The piano concertos can also be considered in this division, Nos. 1 and 2 coming under the early heading, 3, 4 and 5 as middle period works. It is an interesting classification, although it contains the disadvantages of any arbitrary grouping.

It is easy to trace external influences in the first sonatas Op. 2. In No. 1 in F minor, Beethoven began where Mozart left off; the device of raising a theme a tone or semitone, often used by Beethoven to express urgency or tension has already been noted in Haydn. Mozart had been content to repeat a theme in the dominant, even in the taut first movement of the Sonata in C minor (K491). Clementi's fondness for double thirds and sixths, broken octaves is echoed in the Sonata in C Major Op. 2, No. 2.

After the sonatas of Op. 2 however, one is not so conscious of derivative influences. From the Sonata in E flat major Op. 7 on, the voice is unmistakably that of Beethoven. Intensity of feeling is not lacking in the first period sonatas— in the tragic introduction to the 1st movement of Op. 13, the slow movements of Op. 10, No. 3 and Op. 2, No. 2. The sonatas of Op. 27 with their sub-headings *quasi una fantasia* point to the coming freedom of the middle period works. There is an improvisatory quality in the first movements of both these sonatas which shows an imaginative approach to sonata form.

This freedom is immediately noticeable in the first sonatas of the middle period. The first movement of Op. 31, No. 3 in E flat major plunges and rises with the joyous flight of a bird. The G major Sonata's first movement (Op. 31, No. 1) is facetious, a frequent mood of Beethoven's in this key. The last movement has a Viennese or Schubertian *insouciance*. But the most individual of this set is the second in D minor, particularly in the dual motive of calm followed by agitation in the opening subject of the first movement. The last movement has a rhythmic continuity from beginning to end, twisting and turning like a chain of dancers.

The major works of this period, Opus 53 and Opus 57 are pianists' test pieces. The contrast in mood between the two sonatas is striking, sunlit woodland of the Rhineland (Op. 53) becoming towering chasms and precipices of the underworld in Op. 57. The latter, for all its breadth, is a peculiarly pianistic work. It would be very difficult to make an orchestral version of it, as Weingartner did with the Sonata in B flat major, Op. 106.

The first movement of Op. 53 is usually played too fast. The opening motive lies in a very thick part of the contemporary piano's strings, and needs to be treated very carefully to suggest by an adequate pianissimo the mystery of sunrise in a forest. Tempo is also most important in Op. 57, the final section of the last movement having a much more effective urgency if the movement's basic tempo is kept in check, as marked. It is hard to take much interest in the Sonata in F. major, Op. 54 sandwiched between these two. It never seems to come to life, but remains dry and academic.

The later sonatas of this period are slighter works in dimension also, sometimes harking back to the first period in texture, though not in spirit. The angry young man has become more philosophical. Opuses 78, 81a, and 90 could not have been written in the first period, yet they are free from the middle period's '*sturm und drang*'. The calm of the first movement of Op. 78 in F sharp major is mature. In its romantic colour it is true nineteenth century piano writing. The concentration and control of the second movement are the result of years of piano composition. These sonatas stand in relief to the storms of Op. 53 and Op. 57, a relaxation or pause for breath before the intensity of the late period sonatas. They are on a par with the 8th Symphony; Op. 79 is a trifle, Beethoven G major fun, with a curious Barcarolle in the minor key for a central movement.

We can only stand silent before the perfection of the last five sonatas. They are the Valhalla of piano composition, the twilight of sonata form. No piano music has reached their heights. In their sublimity they remain inviolate on a metaphysical plane. It is impossible to 'teach' anyone these sonatas. The first movement of Op. 101 must be 'discussed' rather than played. If the player is to succeed he must have an innate understanding of the style of this period of Beethoven's composition, an intuitive feeling for it.

In this elusive first movement, mere lyricism is not enough; it will fail entirely if there is not tautness as well. The physical world of the earlier two periods has now been left behind, and no earth-bound pianist should attempt these sonatas.

Formally the sonata is stretched to its utmost limits in the last period. When a fugue or fugato passage appears, it is not so much its architectural shape which is impressive, as in a Bach fugue, but its tension (Op. 101 last movement) its spiritual escalation (Op. 110 last movement) or its sweep (Op. 106). In Op. 110 Beethoven felt his treatment of fugue form was in keeping with the nineteenth century, viz. the bold breaking off in the middle for an emotional recall of the Arioso. At the re-appearance of the fugue's subject, demonstration of fugal devices, inversion, diminution and augmentation fade before the transcendental calm which has now settled over the movement. The gradual resumption of the fugue's former impetus is no ordinary fugal final section, but a mysto-rhapsodical conclusion in which listener and player are lifted out of themselves into a state of ecstatic contemplation.

Variation form takes on a new plane of existence in the variations of the last movements of Opuses 109 and 111. In the central movement of Op. 57 the variations moved a stage further than those in the early sonatas Op. 14, No. 2 and Op. 26, by expressing spiritual elevation in their gradual rise from the bass of the theme through the compass of the piano. But the harmonic and metrical pattern is clearly visible in the change from the crotchet chords of the theme to the quaver, semiquaver and demisemiquaver subdivision. In the variations in the last sonatas the theme undergoes an apotheosis.

If there is no comparison of the musical content of the last sonatas with that of the earlier periods, there are occasional similarities of harmony or construction. Certain harmonic procedures are common to the first movements of the Sonatas in A flat major of Op. 26 and Op. 110. Not only are the moods of each opening subject related, but so are the harmonies. In Variation 1 of Op. 26 the simplicity of the demisemiquavers blossom out in a fine tracery of sound covering the whole keyboard in the bridge passage of the first movement of Op. 110.

The *adagio* and *allegro* of the first movement of the Sonata in C minor Op. 111 had already been forecast in the first movement of Op. 13 in C minor, although the later work is titanic rather than pathetic. From the minor clashes of this movement comes a resolution into C major calm from which the *Adagio* second movement arises. In its concluding pages piano music comes closest to Nirvana. Here in the realization of a great interpretation we are suspended in time and space in ultimate nothingness.

CHAPTER 4

THE GOLDEN AGE OF PIANO COMPOSITION

The major developments in the history of the pianoforte occurred from 1800–1880, and it was during this century that the most wonderful piano music was written. Over this period the instrument gradually increased in length, breadth and volume. Its slender, elegant harpsichord shape became more and more solid. At first it was an instrument of some romantic charm, suited to accompany the lyrics of Thomas Moore, or to sigh over the Nocturnes of Field and Chopin. As it acquired more power it became an orchestra in itself, retaining a satisfactory balance between strength and sweetness until the middle of the twentieth century. How much of its singing quality has been lost is evident when a present-day pianist begins the accompaniment of a song such as Richard Strauss's Morgen. The hard steely sound of the contemporary piano is no longer a match for the voice. But in the nineteenth century it was still a singing instrument. The skilful player of a Nocturne could convey the illusion of singer and accompanist by balance of tone between right and left hands, while pivotal notes of the bass harmonies gave off delicate overtones by means of the sustaining pedal.

In the nineteenth century the piano acquired a popularity never attained by harpsichord or clavichord, whose background had been more exclusive. Now the musical milieu became bourgeois, the piano a middle-class instrument for

125

the drawing-room. There is an amusing portrait of Chopin playing to a group of ladies (amongst them George Sand) all striking appropriately soulful attitudes. Like some of the young ladies, music began to get the vapours. To his annoyance Chopin's Nocturnes appeared in the first English edition with sub-titles of Tears, Sighs, or Lamentations. Later there was more mawkish sentimentality when inferior pieces such as The Maiden's Prayer or Remembrance became fashionable.

During this nineteenth Century the piano's increasing strength made it a suitable instrument for the 'grand manner.' Pianists wore manes of hair (their own), in contrast to the formal perukes of their eighteenth Century predecessors. Liszt was caricatured in *La Vie Parisienne* in 1886, with as many arms as an Indian God, shattering a piano to pieces. An umbrella handy to help him, he is wearing the sword of honour presented to him by Hungary, 'but he has ceased to use it as he finds he can hurt the piano more with his hands alone'. The iron-framed piano now had the resilience to withstand this powerful attack. As the rhyme had it, 'The Abbé Liszt banged the piano with his fist.' But the romantic piano could whisper in twilight reverie, as well as thunder heroically.

The foundations of piano technique having been laid by a number of pioneers whose studies are still essential to to-day's pianist, a group of great romantic composers was born 1809–11, Chopin, Schumann, Mendelssohn and Liszt; Beethoven was in his forties, Schubert in his teens. They were followed by another great (if sterner) Romantic, Johannes Brahms, whose compositions would be unthinkable on any but the iron-framed piano. Like Beethoven these composers were unhampered by any ambiguity between harpsichord and piano. With the exception of Schumann they were fine performers, but no doubt considered themselves as composers first and players second. Later in the century the emphasis shifted to the player in the case of pianist-composers such as Busoni, Paderewski or Godowsky.

Frédéric Chopin (1810–49)

From a purely pianistic standpoint, Chopin remains the greatest piano composer i.e. he produced the most mellifluous sounds from the instrument. The piano of Chopin's day was much shallower in its touch and not nearly so demanding physically as ours. In his lifetime it acquired metal strengthening as the iron braces in the frame of the Broadwood he played in 1848 in London testify. Although he was not of great physical strength, his bigger music is as tough and masculine in its fire, as anyone else's.

The studies alone can daunt the strongest pianist, particularly on our heavy piano. The major difficulties of piano technique are to be found in them, dealt with in such an artistic way that we can forget their technical purpose and enjoy them as pieces of music. Played as mere exercises they are boring. They are imaginative studies in touch, tone and velocity and, written between 1829 and 1836, are all the more remarkable as early works.

Romantic composers never hesitated to express their feelings, to wear their hearts on their sleeves. Small wonder that Chopin's Nocturnes have a tremulously feverish quality at times, an expression of the exile's homesickness, the consumptive's anxiety.

To the years 1836–39 belong some of his most despairingly Romantic compositions, the Preludes and the Second Sonata in B flat minor. Here are the musical counterparts of Delacroix's painting of Hamlet, of his portrait of Chopin, a mixture of artistic sensitivity and anguish.

The B flat minor Sonata centres around the *Funeral March* (1837), the other movements (1839) leading up to and away from it. It might be a portrait of a young Romantic hero. Despair, love and triumph figure in the first movement. The Scherzo's dark undercurrent of bitterness and fatality is relieved in the tender melody of the trio, by a vision of the beautiful beloved, a vision that is recalled in the coda of the movement, before the pianissimo left hand octaves ring down the curtain on the young man's life. Bowed heads and mourners' grief are conveyed in the funeral march, muffled drums and flags fluttering in the bleak sunshine of an autumn day. The procession pauses, and in Max Beerbohm's words, the 'soul of the departed friend' speaks in the supremely moving aria which is the trio. The cryptic last movement with its whirling triplets of quavers seems more like the soul's journey out of the world than Chopin's cynical description of it as 'chattering after the funeral'. Romantic fatalism received no truer expression in piano music than in this sonata, from the descending octaves at the outset to the defiant chords at the close. Only in some of the Preludes (1836–38) did Chopin make such a direct expression of grief.

The Third Sonata in B minor (1844) is on a much higher emotional plane, prouder in its defiance, more objective. Not only is there the difference between the two minor keys, the one flat, the other sharp, in the first movements, but in this sonata's opening movement there are many joyous or rhapsodic major episodes, which give it an entirely different character. The radiant cantabile second subject is Chopin at his most expansively melodic. The mercurial Scherzo in E flat major, has none of the earlier sonatas's forebodings in its E flat minor Scherzo, only sparkling sunshine. No tears either in the B major slow movement, but rich melodic warmth. The proud last movement has tremendous drive which never flags for a moment.

It would be difficult to find more ardently passionate pieces in the whole of keyboard music than the four Chopin Ballades. Wessel in his first English edition of them explained that these 'ballades' are without words, but he could not resist subtitling the youthful G minor Ballade Op. 23 (completed in 1835) *La Favorite,* and the second *Ballade La Gracieuse,* both wholly unsuitable titles.

The first Ballade, most overtly dramatic of the four, tells its musical story the most vividly. The arresting introduction puts us back in the Middle Ages, in the era of knightly chivalry and romance. After a sombre narrative of tragic bygone events, hunting horns (fourths and fifths) introduce a tender melody in E flat major, perhaps the image of the knight's adored lady. This theme is expanded triumphantly first into A major, then later more impetuously over swirling quavers, in its original key. In the whole of this central section there are great vivacity and exhilaration. But the stark motto opening theme re-appears, and there is a final charge into battle, defiance and death.

The Second Ballade was completed on a tiny upright piano during Chopin's unhappy stay in Majorca in 1839. It has two contrasting main elements: a serenely placed landscape in its principal theme, shattered by an avalanche of sound.

If any Ballade were to be called *La Gracieuse* it should surely have been the third in A flat major written in the following year. It is the only tale of happiness among them. Here are no violent changes of key, but a succession of sunny themes in major tonalities, only momentarily obscured by the C sharp minor episode of scurrying clouds before the burst of radiance on the concluding page.

With its eloquent 'once upon a time' opening we are once again back in the past in the fourth Ballade in F minor (1842). Although the narrative thread and dramatic impact are not so strong as in the first Ballade, here is the most richly beautiful pianistic writing of the four. In further compensation there is melodic beauty, and a profusion of lush ornate figuration. The deluge of sound of the closing pages is among the most thrilling of all Chopin finales, broken off dramatically by four stark chords.

The four Scherzi must be the boldest of their kind in all music, bitter jokes, grandly dramatic. Formally they are more concisely knit than the ballades, fitting into a broad ternary plan. All are quick-moving with contrasted slower middle sections. So diabolic is its main section that No. 1 in B minor (1831–2) has had the title *Le Banquet Infernal* given it. The contrasting middle section, based on a Polish carol, mocks it gently. No. 2 in B flat minor (1837) is all romantic pride and gesture. The broadly heroic third Scherzo in C sharp minor (1839) has a quietly beautiful second theme answered by shimmering cascades of descending quavers, rare laughter among the Scherzi. The fourth in E major (1842) has a quiet air of fatalism, but becomes fiercely Slavonic in its coda. Biggest in canvas of all the independent pieces is the Fantasie in F minor, which retains the improvisatory nature of a fantasia in spite of its monumental over-all formal structure. The solemn introduction is a quasi-funeral march. It gives way to agitation and unrest which are sometimes relieved by delightfully carefree episodes in contrasting major keys. There is a central section whose peaceful calm is a perfect foil to the surrounding turmoil. The triumphal march at the conclusion of the first part (the over-all scheme being broadly ternary) is heard again at the end before a dramatic downrush of triplet quavers. Then there is a quiet solo recitative of affecting stillness before the curtain is rung down over a murmuring rising flood of triplets. The drama concludes with two defiant chords.

Pride and fearless courage are the essence of the national music, the Mazurkas and Polonaises. They epitomize Polish chivalry, courage in the face of death or danger.

On the other hand the salon pieces—Impromptus, Waltzes, Berceuse or Ecossaises—are relaxed, elegantly graceful. The late Barcarolle (1845–6) is moving in its poignancy. The concluding pages of the lovers in the gondola vowing eternal faithfulness are heart-rending in their nostalgia. There is a shimmering coda, and the work is typically dismissed in plain octaves.

Chopin is often badly served by those 'interpreters' who bestow a false sentimentality on his music. Although rubato and elasticity are essential in many of his compositions, there must be an underlying beat for rubato to make its effect. To distort his music by continually pulling it out of shape is a false application of elasticity. A piece of elastic may be stretched to the full, but when released reverts to its original length.

That Chopin had regard for classical line is evident from his sonatas, which have more symmetry than other romantic sonatas. They have more formal unity than some of the late Beethoven movements, certainly more sense of structure than the Gothic revival 'follies' of Liszt's Sonatas or the Schumann *Fantasie*.

Robert Schumann (1810–56)

Enthusiasm and impetuosity are the most notable character-istics of Schumann, not only in his own music, but in his appreciation of that of others. His effervescent vitality was balanced by an introspective calm, the turbulent Florestan. of the Carnaval as opposed to the reflective Eusebius. He had an appreciation of poetic beauty in terms of the pianoforte similar to that of Chopin, in atmospheric pieces such as Des Abends or in the portrait of Chopin in the Carnaval.

No less of a romantic than Chopin, his music does not always lie as easily under the hand. He was less reserved too in giving his pieces fanciful titles, although often only after they had been composed. Apart from the Sonatas and the Fantasie Op. 17, most of his piano music consists of collections of small pieces or variations—the Fantasy pieces, Carnaval, Kreisleriana, Scenes from Childhood, Abegg variations, Etudes Symphoniques etc. It was the vignette, the kaleidoscope which appealed to him: Scenes Mignonues à la Carnaval—delicate visions flashing past one after the other in rapid succession, like his own bubbling enthusiasms; Traumes Wirren, dream shapes from his own world of fantasy, fantasy pieces of a life which ended in the nightmare hallucinations of mental illness.

His major piano achievement is the Fantasie Op. 17. There is tremendous expansion in the broadly declamatory first section, typically wild enthusiasm in the March (cf. the Davidsbündler March in the Carnaval), then calm in the final section. In the arch in which Schumann envisaged this work there are three sides of his life and musical personality—Florestan, David and Eusebius. His music glows with an enveloping warmth, an impetuous enthusiasm which carries all before it, like the opening of the A minor Piano Concerto. Then he melts us disarmingly with tender affectionate melody.

Felix Mendelssohn—Bartholdy (1809–47)

Mendelssohn, whose piano works suffer an unjustifiable neglect at the present time, showed precocious gifts as a youth, by composing the Midsummer Night's Dream music at the age of sixteen. This work gives the key to all Mendelssohn in its gaiety, lightness, and the melodic charm which was later to find an outlet in the songs, and the Songs

Without Words for piano.

Mendelssohn's romanticism was not so literary as Schumann's, so melancholy as the Keatsian expression of Chopin. In its appreciation of natural beauty it was Wordsworthian—the *Hebrides Overture*, the impish nocturnal frolics of Shakespeare's fairy world.

Franz Liszt (1811–1886)

The most flamboyantly romantic of the nineteenth century composers, Liszt lived his romanticism as well as composing it. He was one of the few musicians who expressed himself as much in his life as in his music. Liszt has been derided and misunderstood as a composer. Even today when increasing interest is being shown in his work, he is still not given his due by those who set themselves up as Liszt players. The worst qualities of Liszt's music are brought out when it is vulgarized or sensationalized. There are musical and noble qualities in it as well as noise and flashiness.

How rarely are the Petrarchan Sonnets played with appreciation of the words of the poems! They might as well be a catalogue of the Army and Navy Stores for all that their romantic ardour is realized by many pianists. No. 47 is a warm benediction on the beloved, recalling the first meeting. No. 104 has a tension in its burning passion that can scarcely be controlled:

> Warfare I cannot wage, yet know not peace,
> I fear, I hope, I burn, I freeze again.
> Mount to the skies, then bow to earth my face,
> Grasp the whole world, yet nothing can obtain.
> (Nott's translation)

No. 123 is a rapturous description of the beloved. 'An angel appeared on earth, nature stopped breathless to listen to her tale.' It is typical of Liszt that these pieces appeared in several versions before their final form. Originally songs, they were written for piano and later revised. In an ideal edition the original songs would be printed alongside the keyboard versions.

If an understanding of the 'programme' behind this music is essential to its realization, it is the same with nearly everything Liszt wrote, as there is usually a pictorial, emotional or literary association. Even the concert studies have sub-titles such as 'A Sigh' or 'The Lament', the kind of explicitness to which Chopin fastidiously objected.

Romanticism was matched by religion in Liszt's life. The wonderfully colourful Jeux d'eaux à la Villa de 'Este, forerunner of impressionism on the piano, has a quotation from St. John at the climactic point: 'The water I shall give you will be the water of Life'. Among the specifically religious pieces, St. Francis of Assisi Preaching to the Birds is particularly successful in its piano imagery, the carolling of the bird choir as it rises in the shape of the Cross, the humble piety of St. Francis. St. Francis of Paul walking on the waves is meaningless unless the player is aware of the sense of miracle. There is a march-like passage at the climax (as so often in Liszt) which must be handled very carefully if it is to escape vulgarity.

The heroics in Liszt must be distinguished from the tawdry. The Hungarian Rhapsodies are based on passionate gypsy songs, but few players make us aware of them. In our times Horowitz has all the requisites of the Liszt player, although his pre-second World War Liszt playing was more at the service of romanticism than that of his latter years, when he has lived in America, and the virtuoso seems to have eclipsed the musician.

Liszt's romanticism was Byronic in its demonstrativeness. The early works up to 1848, when he retired from the concert platform to devote himself seriously to composition, were mainly flamboyant transcriptions or early versions of pieces to be revised in his maturity, viz. the *Album d'un Voyageur* which became the *Années de Pélérinage*. To the Weimar days belongs the Sonata in B minor (1852), a Faustian portrayal of the battle between good and evil. No mere technical dexterity will suffice in the presentation of this colossal merger of music drama and keyboard athletics. Liszt is most true to his dual self here, Mephistopheles and Faust in one.

In the last fifteen years of his life there was an astonishing change in his style of writing. It is hard to recognize the earlier Liszt in the late pieces, which are no longer flamboyant, but spare, at times stark.

Liszt's restlessness was that of the Hungarian gypsies whose music was the basis for the nineteen Rhapsodies. From his ceaseless round of concerts in Europe as a young man until his old age, he was constantly travelling, apart from the comparatively fixed period at Weimar. He was 'drunk with life', and did not always show the cool detachment from the form or content of his works as other composers have done. Perhaps being so passionately involved, it was difficult for him to see his works from the outside.

Johannes Brahms (1833–97)

Johannes Brahms sounds a deeper, more serious note than his contemporaries. As was said of his pre-occupation with melancholy themes: 'Brahms is never so happy as when composing about the grave.' In some of his pieces, particularly in those of his last years, there is a feeling of personal complaint, prophetic of Mahler. Like Chopin he hid his feelings behind abstract titles, such as Intermezzo or Capriccio. His style of piano playing was massive. As a young man, people trembled when he sat down at the piano, such was his reputation for power. His early works, up to 1862, had tremendous energy, fire and temperament. More than his contemporaries he was keenly interested in the classical forms of fugue, sonata and variation.

In his middle years there is still evidence of great virtuosity. There is more mellowness too. The first lyrical Capriccio and Intermezzos (Op. 76) appear and the Two Rhapsodies (B minor and G minor).

Op. 116–119 are Brahm's twilight pieces. His last work for piano, the E flat Rhapsody Op. 119 returns optimistically to the onward surge and drive of his youth. Yet it ends on a minor note. The supremely beautiful Intermezzo in A major, Op. 118 has a bitter-sweet quality. There are some acute cries from the heart among these pieces — the Intermezzo in A minor, Op. 118 for instance and that in E flat minor from the same set, with its powerful, grief-laden climax.

After Beethoven, Brahms is the biggest of the nineteenth century keyboard composers. His music has a North German seriousness tempered by Viennese charm and it fairly bristles with technical difficulty.

CHAPTER 5

FRENCH PIANO MUSIC

Other countries may have produced more intellectual or more emotional music, but none can rival the imaginative, delicately-colourful compositions for the piano of Debussy and Ravel. These composers require a pianist endowed with exceptionally sensitive fingers. They also need a piano capable of a varied tone-palette. The contemporary instrument in its iron hardness, its black-and-white tonal definitions is not suitable for them.

French music is the antithesis of German, yet paradoxically in our time one of the greatest players of French impressionistic piano music was the German, Walter Gieseking. He spent his formative boyhood years in France, which may have given him an appreciation of French culture and the style of its piano playing. Only someone whose tone production suits this music will be able to play it with any finesse. For finesse is its prime characteristic.

Charles Burney on his travels in Europe 1771–72 considered that French harpsichord players were the finest. Clear texture and appreciation of fine sound were a feature of these *claveçin* composers. Debussy and Ravel inherited their ultra-sensitivity to tone-colour, from the greatest of them, Rameau and Couperin. Both paid them tributes, Debussy in his *Hommage à Rameau,* Ravel in *Le Tombeau de Couperin.*

French composers, in common with the current fashion, changed from *claveçin* to piano, in the 1770s. Minor composers wrote pieces for the new pianoforte, but nothing note was to appear for another eighty years. During this time the piano manufacturers Erard and Pleyel were making important contributions to the instrument's development, but in composition the romantic idols of nineteenth century France were Chopin from Poland, and Liszt from Hungary. There was unfortunately no equivalent of Berlioz for the piano.

The first major piano composer in France was also not a Frenchman, César Franck (1822–90). In his major works for piano solo, the Prélude, Chorale and Fugue, and the Prélude, Aria and Finale, it is obvious that Franck was primarily an organist. They might be piano works composed and played from the organ loft. They showed several fusions of style, organ and piano, religious and secular, Roman Catholic and Protestant. In the Prelude, Chorale and Fugue, Franck the Roman Catholic organist and piano-composer is writing in an extension of a form that, at its best, had been the exclusive province of the Protestant organist, Bach. With romantic freedom, Franck gives it an expansion highly suitable to the piano.

In the concerted and chamber works which involve the piano (e.g. the Quintet in F minor, the Violin and Piano Sonata, the Variations Symphoniques for piano and orchestra) the piano has a more idiomatic rôle, sounds a more subjective pleading note.

Camille Saint-Saëns (1835–1921) made a magnificent contribution to piano technique, but could not handle larger forms as successfully as Franck. His musical style was too superficial, although he came close to Franckian organ breadth in the sole opening of his second Piano Concerto which is a pastiche of Bach. The competent pianist, trained on Saint-Saens studies would finish with a formidable technical equipment. Occasionally they hint at impressionism, as in *Les Cloches de Las Palmas*, Op. 111.

Gabriel Fauré (1845–1924) was a far more sensitive artist, whose delicate gifts found their happiest expression in his songs. Although they come close to fin-de-siècle decadence at times, his piano works could have more attention from pianists. The writing is often complex in its lay-out.

It is a quieter type of virtuosity than that of Saint-Saens, more a Chopinesque fine tracery of sound than a diamond brilliance.

The thirteen Nocturnes are Fauré's most distinctive piano pieces. They are much more extended than the Chopin Nocturnes and, in their meanderings, sometimes seem to sprawl. Like Schubert, Fauré, once started, seems to find it difficult to stop. The Seventh Nocturne in C sharp minor has a haunting nostalgia, an inconsolable grief. Relief comes in a light running F sharp major section, which has some delightful part-writing, and is sheer joy in the hands of a pianist with an eye and ear for tone-colour. After a return to the sombre mood of the opening, there is a quiet D flat major close based on material of the happier Allegro section. Grief is assuaged, resolved.

The fifth Nocturne in D flat major explores the piano's possibilities of sustained melodic beauty, in a ripe fullness of sound not even achieved by Chopin. The contrasting section is first of grave, elegiac beauty reminiscent of his song-cycle to Verlaine's poems, *La Bonne Chanson*. Then follows a soaring melody over a lightly-flying semiquaver accompaniment. The fourth Nocturne in E flat major (a good introduction to Fauré's singing poised style of piano-writing) is much more conventional, but far less subtle.

The Barcarolles are elegant, undulating and flowing. The 1st in A minor is a sad love-song sung by the gondolier. There is a wonderfully liquid central section, which floats along. Truly Fauré had the secret of extracting beautiful sounds from the pianoforte, in which to couch his beautiful melodies. The Impromptus are 'sewing-machine' music demanding nimble fingers. A deeper note of pathos is sounded in the Theme and Variations (Op. 73). Fauré's piano music is of such fragrance and elegant beauty that it will never become vulgarised or popularised. In its wistful appeal it is not unlike the painting of Renoir. Much of it is cast in the half-light of *fin-de-siècle* French songwriters such as Reynaldo Hahn, *l'heure exquise,* when flowers glow in the twilight with an unnatural beauty, after the heat of a summer's day. Perhaps this transience best describes the relationship of Fauré's music to the main 'day' of music. But it is nonetheless piercingly radiant for all that.

It is as wide of the mark to call Fauré the French Schumann as it is to compare Saint-Saéns with Liszt. Fauré is as serene as Schumann is impetuous; Saint-Saëns however prodigious his virtuosity, has not the romantic ardour of Liszt.

As if to make up for the lack of French interest in sonata form, or the bigger Teutonic musical structures, Paul Dukas (1865–1935) wrote an interminable piano sonata, whose size is more notable than its musical content. It is a huge tasteless neo-Gothic 'folly'. French musical temperament does not lend itself to the lugubrious epic, but prefers brevity and wit.

With the compositions of Claude Debussy (1862–1918) and Maurice Ravel (1875–1937) at the end of the century, French piano writing acquired an imaginative distinction which it has not reached since. The usual practice of coupling these composers together, 'Debussy and Ravel', while admitting their contemporary brilliance, fails to distinguish between their very dissimilar qualities. To many people their work is as far as they need go in twentieth century piano music. In one respect they are right, for no one has written in such grateful piano style, or rather styles, since. They are the last great writers in the nineteenth century tradition of pianistic elegance and taste.

The appeal of French music at the turn of the century is essentially to the senses. It is to be savoured as the bouquet of a very fine wine, to be enjoyed principally for its sensuous beauty. In the visual arts, whose creators were much more numerous, a corresponding response to colour was evident, for instance, in the painting of Monet, Sisley, Pissarro and Gauguin.

In this specialised world of fine sound, Debussy occupies a special world of his own in French music. He was not interested in the percussive possibilities of the piano, aiming to create the illusion that the piano has no hammers. Debussy was feline by nature; velvet paws concealed the claws in his music.

The early piano pieces e.g. the Reverie (1890), were

reminiscent of Massenet (1842–1912) whose sugary melodies influenced most of his contemporaries with their faded charm. Every French composer of this period is said to have a little of Massenet in him. But Debussy soon found a more individual, sophisticated expression, as startling a change as between the early conventional paintings of Gauguin and those from Tahiti. Debussy's mature piano pieces (1903 *Estampes*) have a similar exotic sensuousness (*Pagodes, Soirée dans Grenade, Jardins sous la Pluie*).

It is difficult for the contemporary pianist to penetrate into Debussy's magic world of sound, the music of suggestion, of half-lights, vague undertones and languour. On the contemporary piano it is like illuminating the shadowy forest of Pelléas and Mélisande with searchlights or neon signs. It is an instrument to be struck, not cosseted, on which to shout, not murmur. There has never been a composer who treated the piano with such intimacy, and his music needs a pre-1939 piano at least. The two Books of Preludes (1910–13), his monumental achievement in piano imagery, need the magic fingers and piano of a Cortot to bring them to life. Even more elusive are the accompaniments to the songs.

Debussy was not only a composer of exotic music. His qualities could portray the child's world with subtle delineation. Not even Schumann can rival his excursion into the nursery, in the delightful humour of the *Childrens' Corner Suite*.

Maurice Ravel was more objective. He had the French qualities of balance, logic and good taste in his music, but in spite of a lavish keyboard imagery, not Debussy's hedonistic love of lush sound. His music was extrovert, Debussy's was more inward-looking. Ravel would express pictures and Debussy, moods, as well as pictorial music. He was not such a specifically pianistic composer as Debussy, but often transferred a piece into an orchestral version.

Ravel writing a liquid piece such as *Jeux d'eau*, confines himself to the external scenes of water-play, the splashing fountains, cascading of water. Debussy takes a calm lake on a grey day in *Reflets dans l'eau*, and gives a stillness of mood only broken by mild ruffling of the water by the wind.

Erik Satie (1866–1925) wrote enigmatic pieces which sometimes have a Debussy-like imagery of sound, tempting Debussy to orchestrate two of the three *Gymnopédies*. In the orchestral version they lack the intimacy of the original piano pieces.

In the post first World War period French music became more flippant, in keeping with that of other countries. Francis Poulenc (1899–1969) composed with an impudent wit and even Ravel was influenced by the jazz of the '20s in his G major Concerto (1931). After the second World War it put on a heavy mentle of seriousness in the works of Olivier Messiaen (b. 1908) which sometimes borders on pretentiousness as in the *Vingt Regards sur l'enfant Jésus*. Although his music retains the French respect for neatness of texture, his long-windedness is un-French. Preoccupied with religion, Messiaen has also written extensively on birds, like the early *clavecinistes*, particularly Couperin, and explored Indian music in the *Canteyodjaya*, a serial treatment of rhythm.

Another heavily intellectual composer, Pierre Boulez (b. 1926), is not interested in writing for the piano in any ingratiating style. His third piano sonata is an attack on piano and eardrums, sounding like the impact of plate glass upon concrete. Both Messiaen and Boulez are ideal composers for the contemporary piano.

CHAPTER 6

PIANO COMPOSITION IN THE TWENTIETH CENTURY

The piano is not a satisfactory medium for contemporary composition. In the 150 years that have elapsed since it was first written for in 1770, its possibilities have been so well explored that it would be difficult for the contemporary composer to improve on them. The sounds that he is now seeking do not belong to it, so he alters it, 'prepares' it by the insertion of screws, rubbers, pencils; anything to pervert its tone. He likes to use extremes of treble and bass. The combination of these does not sound very attractive, but he is not looking for beautiful sound, so it does not matter.

The contemporary composer is attracted by high-pitched sounds as eerie as the wind whistling through telephone wires, as euphonic as ships straining at their hawsers in port, trains shunting on rusty iron rails. These noises are more easily expressed by electronic means, or by setting stretched strings in motion by a bow, by thumping on surfaces of stretched hide, than by banging on the piano, whose powers of percussion and pitch are feeble compared with mechanical or orchestral possibilities.

One point stands out in contemporary music. It lacks a unified style. Whereas the most prominent nineteenth century composers (seen from the distance of our century) appear to have certain romantic characteristics in common, a harmonic language which is consistent, an idiom of writing which is easily recognizable, in the twentieth century the main stream of music has divided into several tributaries, so different are the various styles and technique of writing.

Some American writers have attempted to classify these different currents but it is still too soon to get a clear view of the situation. Among the mass of those who are writing music in any period, there may be six great composers who remain for posterity. Perhaps the idiom, the technique of writing is not so vitally important after all. What does matter is whether a composer has anything to say. In his *Lukas Passion*, Penderecki uses many different techniques of twentieth century composition, but it is such an overwhelmingly beautiful work that the techniques are forgotten. Only the result is important.

In spite of differing techniques, contemporary composers have certain features in common. They scorn obvious melodic beauty. That is left to the 'pop' composers. They prefer producing harsh to mellifluous sounds, disjointed rather than flowing effects. They do not appear to be particularly interested in proportion, prefer to avoid a regular rhythmic pulse, as they avoid recognizable tonality. They seem to prefer understatement to enthusiasm.

All these are opposite to the qualities which appealed to the nineteenth century. It liked melody, rhythm and warmth. The response to nineteenth century piano music seemed more universal. It was played by many pianists. Early piano recitalists played only current compositions. Now the appeal of contemporary music is more limited, and often a composer has one particular interpreter who is the main performer of his works (Messiaen: Yvonne Loriod, Stockhausen: Kontarsky, Henze: Eschenbach).

One wonders whethers a contemporary work which appeals to many different pianists may not have more ultimate value e.g. Michael Tippett's second Piano Sonata (1962) which is in the repertoire of many pianists, at least of many English pianists.

Music has now become an intellectual exercise. It is not to be enjoyed. Heaven help the composer who writes an 'enjoyable' work. He will immediately be pounced on by the critical fraternity as being out of tune with the times. Music is now supposed to torture us if it is to be worthwhile, to be part of the fashionable wave of masochism. In the

enormous material advancement of the twentieth century
we have lost the sense of wonder at the world around us,
and in its matter-of-factness contemporary music is a
faithful expression of this flatness.

Already certain piano composers stand out in the
twentieth century, certain works are landmarks. Alban
Berg's Sonata Op. 1 (1906–8) is valid today as the first
work to approach atonality. It is by no means 'cool', but
has the typical malaise of Viennese composition at the
beginning of the century. It is a remarkable Op. 1 even
though it lacks shape and contrast.

Schönberg turned his back on this neurosis when he
wrote his first 12-tone music for the piano (the five pieces
Op. 23, 1923, and the Suite Op. 25, 1925) reverting to
eighteenth century dance forms for the titles of the various
movements, a perversion when one considers the end-pro-
duct. But Schönberg's quality as a musician is obvious.
His mind is of a greatness that would shine through in
whatever idiom he chose to write.

Stravinsky's sophisticated Sonata (1924) is witty and
elegant in its outer movements. The neo-Bach slow movement is deeply expressive.

Bartok's Sonata (1926) is a work of ebullient percussion.
For all Bartok's pianistic gifts, this work does not lie comfortably under the hand, however stimulating it is to play and
hear. The slow movement aims at producing melodic
effect from the repetition of a single note, and by skilful
harmonic and rhythmic arrangement, makes its effect.
Bartok suffers in the hands of pianists who take an axe
to the keyboard. They have heard that Bartok is a percussive
composer. In an excess of zeal they produce a murderous
tonal effect, which assaults the eardrums. One of Bartok's
most attractive piano works which does not strain the
medium is the third Piano Concerto. Its slow movement
has the timelessness of a Mozart slow movement.

Some composers whose roots were in the nineteenth
century reflected changing fashions in their later works,
or made changes in their own style. Debussy's Etudes
(1915) occasionally showed more asperity than his earlier
works, a more discursive style. Ravel's Piano Concerto in

G major (1931) has a flippancy in tune with the jazz of the '20s and '30s. The melody of the slow movement (written two bars at a time) shows apathy and a distaste for life, the mediaeval deadly sin of 'accidie', made all the more evident by its slow unconscious parody of an interlude at bar 43 of the Prelude from the Prelude, Aria and Finale by César Franck. Rachmaninoff's Paganini Rhapsody (1934) has a brittle dryness and percussion not found in the preceding piano concertos.

The 'prepared piano' sounds in the works of John Cage and others in this genre, resemble Javanese or Balinese music. They are no more new than Debussy's exotic sounds, but Debussy does not need a 'prepared' piano, only 'prepared' fingers.

Stockhausen's mathematical procedures seem to derive from the serious school of Schonberg. He has a predilection for high or low-lying leger lines. Messiaen and Boulez might also be considered in this school, although Messiaen used a visual imagery or association not found in the music of the other two.

The traditional writers in the twentieth century have their roots in nineteenth century processes. Nevertheless they have produced some excellent music which belongs to the twentieth century as much as any of the works of the iconoclastic composers. Some have been prophetic in their later works, viz. Scriabine. Others such as Rachmaninov, Bax, Ireland, Debussy and Ravel have largely remained faithful to their personal style.

Dry-eyed piano composers like Hindemith, Prokofiev and Shostakovitch are in the emotionally arid river-bed of twentieth century music. A number of English composers, Alan Rawsthorne, Peter Racine Fricker and Lennox Berkeley have similar non-emotional styles. Among younger British composers, the Australian Malcolm Williamson has a sense of purpose and shape in his Sonata (1956) not always evident among his contemporaries. Richard Rodney Bennett's Sonata (1954), a precocious work written at age eighteen, has a similar unity of style.

As twentieth century piano composition ignores some of the piano's more likeable qualities, a pianist trained exclusively in it would be at a loss when dealing with the tonal subtleties of nineteenth century music. However the study and performance of twentieth century music can do nothing but good to the pianist brought up on traditional lines. In its concentration on intellectual qualities it gives him a better appreciation of the structural methods of other periods.

It is in contemporary music that the contemporary piano comes into its own. It is the right instrument for it, which vindicates Dr. Neupert's theory of affinity between instrument and the music composed for it. Objective music without particularly tonal subtlety is admirably fitted for the present piano.

The problems of playing contemporary music, with its new system of signs, should encourage publishers to give some elucidation of the text. Composers occasionally write about the performance of their works, as Messiaen, Stockhausen and Cage have done. To the pianist bewildered by different trends at the present time, this cannot be anything but helpful.

Part III

CHAPTER 1

THE MYSTIQUE OF THE PIANO RECITAL

On an empty platform an enormous grand pianoforte, a black stool placed before it. A hall filled with upwards of two thousand people, whose excitement and expectancy are evident in the buzz of their eager chatter. Nothing particularly colourful in the setting, a preponderance of black and white. The heavy jet-black machine, hardly an object of beauty in itself, its black and white keyboard eerie in the glare of bright white light. The darkening of the hall, a sudden hush. The emergence of a celebrated pianist in conventional black and white evening dress, to the accompaniment of frenzied applause. Again, silence. Then white hands begin to extract magical sounds from a mass of ivory, wood and wire; flesh and blood moulding pliant musical phrases from taut steel strings stretched over their iron frame. The wooden hammers embedded in thick felt, acting as agents between fingers and strings to produce sounds of no intelligible language save that which begins 'where speech leaves off'.

Sounds which have no specific meaning in themselves, but different associations for different people; carrying for some, emotional overtones as subtle as the musical overtones given off by the instrument's bass notes; which can move one listener to tears, and leave another, to whom this musical speech is incomprehensible or unfamiliar, completely unmoved.

The silence that descends on an audience when it is

absorbed in music and artist. The thoughtless open coughing which can spoil a performance, an infectious complaint which upsets audience and pianist, the latter listening to the coughs instead of the sounds he is making, the audience restless from the waves of disturbance it creates. The moment of silence at the end of a quiet work, before the release of tension by an outburst of applause, or tumultuous applause which hardly waits for the last note of an exciting piece, sometimes closing over a work before it is finished. Now no longer a series of individuals, but a collective unit, the audience has become an active participant in the music.

Would one of these individuals receive an equivalent sensation from the pianist playing to him in private? The outlines of the music might not be so sharp, the impression so vivid, without the tension created in artist and audience by the sense of occasion. A good deal of the listener's active enjoyment is created by the awareness of the audience around him, the collective concentration, the projection of the pianist's personality. Otherwise he might as well sit at home and listen to one of his gramophone records, or watch him on television. How flat it would seem to an audience if they were merely assembled to listen to a programme of recordings! No heightened perception here, no personal magnetism, just a desire to let thoughts wander, indulge in desultory conversation. The gramophone record is best heard alone, without distraction from others. The world of the record is a private one, in a quiet as hushed as that of the recital audience.

What is the fascination of a piano recital? Piano recitalists outnumber all other solo performing artists, singers, string-players, guitarists and organists. So many young musicians aspire to become pianists. The piano recital is a comparative-ly new form of entertainment not 150 years old. Perhaps its attraction is in the projection of a powerful personality over a sea of assembled humanity. Or maybe, the idea of one man being able to make a piano sound like an orchestra. A surgeon once explained to me that he found piano-playing fascinating because it is an activity in which so many things are co-ordinated: emotions, muscles, brain and nerves. But this would hardly interest the layman. Liszt, the first piano recitalist, seems to have been the Messiah of a new cult, his audience cast under his spell. His present-day disciples are still able in their own way to perform miracles and mesmerize audiences.

No pianist now would aim at making his concert a tour-de-force comparable with that of Liszt. What was once regarded as wizardry would probably be shrugged off today as vulgarity: those flowery fantasias on operatic airs, improvisation on themes submitted, personal flourishes added to a composer here and there. In our time the piano recital is much more serious, more formal, almost clinical. There are no 'assisting artists'. What was once primarily entertainment, even exhibitionism, has become an enterprise which is suspect if there is any air of enjoyment about it. Today's pianist looks very serious, as though he were not enjoying making music at all, or aiming at expressing anything, let alone himself and his philosophy of life.

Yet the personality cult is still the prime factor in a pianist's drawing power, a legend that precedes him, accumulated over the years, or in a startlingly short time by the blaze of publicity media: television, newspaper or gramophone. His position may be equally precarious. As suddenly as the spotlights of the world shine on him, as suddenly they may be switched off, to focus on the latest international prize-winner, whose turn it is to bask, or sweat in the glare of the beacons for a brief moment.

It is a matter for speculation just how much an audience is aware of the quality of a pianist's work, how much its judgment is due to an extraneous factor, to the reputation he has acquired, to the critics who confidently tell the public what it should like. Much goes by the fashion of the moment. A pianist may be in demand, then suddenly be passed over, no longer 'in the swim'. Lucky is the one who can hold his own regardless of current trends.

Different countries admire different kinds of artists. A pianist with a big following on the continent may be dismissed out of hand by the arbiters of taste in England. Music, generally supposed to be a universal language, does not have the same meaning in all countries. It has as many forms of utterance as there are nationalities.

What is it that makes a person become a pianist? Does he feel, like a priest, that he is 'called' to his profession, or is it merely an occupation to him? Is it a wish to assert himself over a mass of people, to be admired, applauded, cheered? Does he still feel Liszt's power of intoxicating an audience? Whatever the reason, the desire to play in public usually comes when quite young and often before he has reached his teens, the future performer is set in his purpose. Let us hope he thinks first of his service to music, to the work and its composer, creating it anew, 're-creating' it.

Some players have a tremendous burst of activity when young, then suddenly disappear, while others consolidate their position over the years. Maybe it is a matter of tenacity, of making every sacrifice for their work. To judge from the fate of the hundreds of aspiring pianists who present themselves before the public every year, in emulation of their seniors, many are 'called', but few 'chosen'. For a recitalist to make his mark, he must have something to say, and a distinctive manner in the saying. Ambition is not enough. Pianists cannot be made to order, like typists, although many play like them. They must be 'committed' and make others share their involvement. The test of an artist is in the reaction to his recital. Are you the same human being who entered the hall? Has he taken you through an uplifting experience?

Even if it is less exotic than in the days of Liszt, still the mystique remains: it is only destroyed in the anti-climax of the artists' room after the concert where among the eager autograph hunters, innumerable inanities are exchanged by artist and admirers.

The next day the commercial-traveller pianist goes forth to roam the globe, the young sometimes in the style of a pop-singer, the older more often resembling a business man. It is not his doing, he is merely conforming to the times in which he lives, instead of rising above them.

CHAPTER 2

PIANO RECITAL PROGRAMMES

Over the years piano recital programmes have changed as much as the instrument itself. They not only mirror the taste of a particular country, a particular audience at a particular period of time, but they also reflect a performer's view of music. The muscular pianist of today may play an esoteric programme, viz. The Hammerklavier Sonata of Beethoven and the Bach Goldberg Variations. Apart from the fact that the latter work is unidiomatic on the piano, two such gigantic works on the one programme is bad planning. It is more a feat of endurance than an artistic enterprise.

The technician jostles all kinds of brilliant music together, regardless of its suitability e.g. the two books of the Paganini Variations of Brahms, Liszt's B. minor Sonata and twelve Chopin Studies. The hack begins with Bach's Chromatic Fantasia and Fugue (in the von Bülow version) followed by the Appassionata Sonata and a Chopin group, a familiar road which is as routined as his playing. A one-composer recital of Beethoven, Chopin or Liszt can be helpful stylistically if the programme is judiciously chosen, and the player has sufficient musicianship to hold our interest. The twelve Transcendental Studies of Liszt in one programme would be supportable if there were a romantic pianist left to carry them through with the required fervour and panache. But in an age when Liszt players are predominantly technicians, a selection of six of the more interesting is quite enough.

153

Very rarely does a pianist take as his theme music written in our time; most ignore it. This is a pity because the main difficulty about twentieth century music is that we do not hear it enough. If the sonatas of Berg, Stravinsky, Boulez or Bartok, were as familiar as those of Beethoven, most of the difficulty would disappear. A well-balanced general programme might surely have some fairly recent compositions as one-third of its content. Many worthwhile earlier composers too are neglected, among them Fauré, Mendelssohn and Tchaikovsky, to name but a few.

After its invention the piano took sixty years to reach the status of a solo instrument. At its first recorded solo performance in 1768 J. C. Bach probably played one of his own sonatas. Pianists continued to play their own music for the next sixty years, although in the early nineteenth century the piano was rarely heard on its own in a concert. Even Liszt had the assistance of singers and instrumentalists in his early concerts.

In London in 1840 he played the Beethoven Kreutzer Sonata with the violinist Ole Bull, and accompanied Rubini in Schubert songs. On his own he played a Händel fugue, and his version of the Overture to Rossini's opera *William Tell*. This varied programme may have been a retort to those who complained he only played his own works.

A highly-acclaimed pianist who mainly played his own compositions or improvisations, Sigismund Thalberg, at a London concert on March 6th, 1848 in conjunction with orchestra and singers, played as solos his arrangement of two of the favourite airs from Bellini's Sonnambula, a Capriccio on the Serenade from *Don Pasquale*, and a Fantasia on the Minuet and Serenade from *Don Giovanni*.

Earlier in the same year Sterndale Bennett, in company with two singers, two violins and celli, paid tribute to the lately deceased Mendelssohn in a programme dedicated to his music. The solo piano performances consisted of a Prelude and Fugue from Op. 35, one of the seven characteristic pieces and some of the Songs without Words.

In the middle of the nineteenth century, piano programmes took on a more serious stereotyped form, and the accompanying artists disappeared. In his *Autobiography* Anton

Rubinstein notes this change after the revolutionary events of 1848, which he says affected artistic tastes in Europe. When pianists such as Von Bülow, Walter Bache and De Pachmann played others' music, as opposed to improvisations or their own compositions, they usually stuck to Beethoven, Chopin and Liszt as staple composers.

Probably the most enterprising keyboard recital programmes given in the nineteenth century were the three series of historical performances 'in strictly chronological order' by Ernst Pauer in London in 1862, 1863 and 1867. For the first series in 1862 Pauer played all the works composed for harpsichord on a harpsichord (a very rare event in the nineteenth century) and reserved the Broadwood pianoforte at his disposal, for the piano compositions. In the third series of 1867, he used a bichorda piano (an early type of piano with two strings to a note) instead of a harpsichord, as many had complained of the harpsichord's thinness of tone. No doubt it was a late eighteenth century harpsichord which would hardly be in good condition in 1862.

The programmes of the 1867 series were:

Wednesday November 27th *1st Concert. Claveçin Works*

Suite in E minor No. 3	Kuhnau
Suite No. 6	Händel
Italian Concerto	J. S. Bach
2 Polonaises	W. F. Bach

Piano Works

Sonata in A major	C.P.E. Bach
Gigue in D minor	Haessler
Fantasia No. 2 in C minor	Mozart
Sonata in F sharp Op. 78	Beethoven
Andante Op. 18	Hummel
Hungarian Rhapsody No. 8	Liszt
Barcarole Op. 6	Thalberg

December 4th *2nd Concert. Claveçin Works*

Allemande Sarabande and Gigue	Lully
Selection of Lessons	Scarlatti

Sonata in D major	Galuppi
Balletto and Gavotte	Martini
Sonata in A major	Paradies

Piano Works

Andante and Presto	Clementi
Selection of Studies	Gramer
Nocturne in A	Field
Nocturne in D flat	Chopin
Arabesque	Schumann
La Triste ⎱ Saltarello ⎰	Heller

December 11th *3rd Concert. Claveçin Works*

La Favorite ⎱ La Tendre Nanette ⎬ La Tenebreuse ⎰	Couperin
Deux Gigues en Rondeaux ⎱ Deux Menuets ⎬ La Poule ⎰	Rameau
Fugue in F major	Krebs
Allegro in E minor	Kirnberger

Piano Works

Andante and Variations in F minor	Haydn
La Consolation	Düssek
Capriccio in G flat	Muller
Andante from Sonata in A flat (Op. 39)	Weber
Rondo in E flat	Weber
Kindermärchen	Moscheles
Impromptu Op. 142, No. 3	Schubert
3 Musical Sketches	Sterndale-Bennett
Allegro Brillant Op. 92 (2 pianos)	Mendelssohn

Anton Rubinstein who on his visits to London was fascinated by Pauer's performance of harpsichord works on the instrument for which they were written emulated Pauer in his historical concerts, but enlarged his series to seven, and used the piano exclusively.

ANTON RUBINSTEIN'S 7 HISTORICAL CONCERTS
1885–86

1st Concert

Byrd	The Carman's Whistle
Bull	The King's jig
Couperin	La Tenebreuse
	Le reveil matin
	La favorite
	Le Bavolet flottant
	La bandoline
Rameau	Le rappel des oiseaux
	La poule
	Gavotte et Variations
Scarlatti	Cat's Fugue
	Sonata, A major
J. S. Bach	Fantaisie Chromatique
	Préludes et Fugues
	Sarabande
	Gavotte
Händel	Fugue, E minor
	Harmonious Blacksmith
	Sarabande
	Passacaille
	Gigue
	Airs et Variations
C. P. E. Bach	Rondo
	La Xenophone
	Sibylle
	Les Langueurs tendres
	La complaisante
Haydn	Thème et Variations
Mozart	Fantaisie C Minor
	Rondo A Minor
	Gigue
	Alla turca

2nd Concert

Beethoven	Sonata C sharp minor op. 27 No. 2
	Sonata D minor Op. 31
	Sonata C major Op. 53

Sonata F minor Op. 57
Sonata E minor Op. 90
Sonata A major Op. 101
Sonata E major Op. 109
Sonata C minor Op. 111

3rd Concert

Schubert   Wanderer fantasie
Moments Musicales 1-6
Menuet H moll
Impromptu C moll

Weber   Sonata A flat
Momento capriccioso
Invitation à la Valse
Polacca E dur

Mendelssohn   Variations sérieuses
Capriccio E dur
11 Songs without words
Presto Capriccio

4th Concert

Robert Schumann   Fantasie C major Op. 17
Kreisleriana (1–8)
Etudes Symphoniques
Sonata Fismoll
Fantasiestücke: Abends
In der Nacht
Traumeswirren
Warum?
Vogel als Prophet
Romanze D moll
Carnaval

5th Concert

Clementi   Sonata B dur
Field   Nocturnes Es dur
A dur
B dur
Hummel   Rondo H moll
Moscheles   3 Etudes caracteristiques
Henselt   Poème d'Amour

	Berceuse
	Liebeslied
	La fontaine
	Schmerz in Glück
	Si oiseau j'étais.
Thalberg	Etude A moll
	Fantaisie über Don Juan
Liszt	Etudes Des
	Valse-Caprice
	Consolations (E dur, Des dur)
	Au bord d'une source
	Rhapsodies hongroises (Nos. 6 and 12)
	Soirées Musicales (Rossini)
	Lieder von Schubert:

Auf dem Wasser zu singen
Ständchen
Erl-konig

Soirées de Vienne, A dur
Fantaisie, Robert le Diable.

	6th Concert
Chopin	Fantaisie F minor
	6 Préludes (E moll, A dur, As dur,
	B moll, Des dur, D moll)

Barcarolle
Valses (As dur
  A dur
  As dur)
Impromptus Fis Ges
Scherzo H moll
Nocturnes Des, G dur, H moll
Mazurkas H moll
  Fis moll
  C dur
  B moll
4 Ballades
Sonata Bb minor
Berceuse
Polonaises (Fis moll
  C minor
  As dur)

160

7th Concert

Chopin	11 Etudes (As dur F moll E dur
	C moll Es moll
	Es dur H moll as dur
	A moll
	Cis moll C moll)

Anton Rubinstein : Sonata F dur
Thème et variation
Scherzo Sonata in A minor

Glinka : Tarantelle
Barcarolle
Souvenir de Mazourka

Balakirev : Scherzo
Mazurka
Islamé

Cui : Scherzo
Polonaise

Tschaikowsky : Chants sans paroles
Valse
Romance
Scherzo a la Russe

Rimsky-Korsakov : Etude
Novelette
Valse

Liadov : Etude
Intermezzo

Nicolas Rubinstein : Feuillet d'Album
Valse

The Queen's Hall in London was the scene of recitals by several great pianists at the turn of the century. A typically traditional late nineteenth century programme was played by Ferruccio Busoni on 23 February 1901:

Prelude and Fugue in D major	Bach-Busoni
Sonata in A flat Op. 26	Beethoven
Sonata in B flat minor	Chopin
2 Studies: Feux Follets ⎱	
Mazeppa ⎰	Liszt
Rhapsodies 13 and 6	Liszt

Ignaz Jan Paderewski played a programme there on June 15th 1897 which would daunt the stoutest-hearted virtuoso. It was that of a young athlete, and is a good example of a young pianist's daring. Like the Rubinstein Series it has the material for two recitals:

Variations and Fugue on a theme by Händel	Brahms
Sonata in D minor Op. 31 No. 2	Beethoven
Carnaval Op. 9	Schumann
Nocturne in B major ⎫ 3 Etudes Op. 25 Nos. 6, 7 and 8 ⎬ Polonaise in A flat major ⎭	Chopin
2 Chants—Polonais, Nos. 1 and 5	Chopin-Liszt
Etude in C major ⎫ Barcarolle in A minor ⎬ Mazurka in D major ⎭	Rubinstein
Rhapsody No. 6	Liszt

At an orchestral concert four days later conducted by 'Mr. Henry Wood,' Paderewski played the Scherzo from Litolff's piano Concerto in D minor, a *morceau* which has become comically familar in our time.

Conventional programmes of predominantly pianistic interest continued up till the first half of the twentieth century. Some survivors of the nineteenth century tradition were still extant, and the piano still had ingratiating qualities of sound. A pianist of the discernment and refinement of Alfred Cortot usually confined his programmes to Romantic or Impressionistic composers, Chopin, Schumann, Liszt, Debussy and Ravel. Nor did one look for unconventionality in the programmes of Sergei Rachmaninov—his magical playing of the familiar composers was enough. His successor Horowitz branched out more boldly into unfamiliar classics, and he has continued this exploration since, although his programmes usually contain a high proportion of technically difficult works, not surprising in such a technically overpowering player.

Today's intelligent pianist usually takes his programme-building very seriously. The Soviet pianists Gilels and

Richter reproduce neglected classics, or reveal new lights on well-known works. A pianist such as John Ogdon has commendably unorthodox views on programme-planning, championing many contemporary composers, or having the courage to give an all-Scriabine recital. Aloys Kontarsky is performing a much-needed musical service in his brilliant expositions of Stockhausen's Piano Pieces.

With the prolixity of pianists piano recitals and recordings at the present time, it is refreshing to find any pianist who does not hesitate to explore new or neglected paths, who reminds us that composers are still writing for the piano.

CHAPTER 3

TRANSCRIPTIONS

Transcription from one musical medium to another is a vexed question among musicians. Some take the view that an arranger commits a felony, but as long as the composer has been dead for 50 years, at least he cannot be prosecuted for breach of copyright. If a composer has sold his work outright, the arranger is likewise free to do his best (or worst) without restriction. There is no need to be too scrupulous on this subject, as there have been so many different kinds of keyboard instruments, so many different types of pianos, that a piece of Bach or Mozart played on the contemporary piano can be considered a transcription in its new setting.

Most composers have indulged in arrangement at some time. Some have been their own arrangers. One of the most 'arranged', J. S. Bach, was adept at the practice himself, transcribing his own compositions or those of others. Purcell, Beethoven, Brahms, Schumann, Debussy and Ravel are a few who have arranged their own or others' pieces. Rachmaninoff made a charming piece out of his song, 'The Lilacs'. When an orchestral score is arranged for the piano it loses a lot of its colour; the reverse process can be equally unsatisfactory through inflation of the original. One of the worst offences in arranging a piano work for orchestra was committed by Humphrey Searle, when he orchestrated the Liszt Sonata in B minor, which was used for the tasteless ballet *Marguerite et Armand*. It is the last of Liszt's piano works which should be orchestrated as it is

163

so idiomatically pianistic. An exception is the Moussorgsky-Ravel *Pictures from an Exhibition,* for Ravel was skilled in making orchestral versions of his own piano pieces. Paradoxically a good arrangement, like a good translation from another language, does not make us aware of the original, but exists in its own right. It would be ideal if the original of an arrangement were printed beside it, so that the player could compare the two.

There are two different motives behind transcription: firstly a genuine interest in or enthusiasm for a work and secondly for commercial 'pop' profit. In our time we are only too aware of the degradation which takes place when themes of Mozart or Tschaikowsky are exploited in the 'pop' field. This is more debasement than arrangement.

The great arranger for the piano is Franz Liszt. Carried away by his genius as a pianist he made numerous arrangements of his own and other people's works, overtures, operas, songs or organ pieces. Liszt could make the piano resound like an orchestra. On one occasion after conducting the Berlioz *March to the Scaffold* he sat down at the piano and played it, giving the impression of producing more volume than the orchestra.

He was particularly fond of his Reminiscences on Meyerbeer's opera, *Robert le Diable.* Once in Paris when he was about to begin the Beethoven Kreutzer Sonata with a violinist, somebody called out from the audience for *Robert le Diable,* whereupon Beethoven was postponed for Meyerbeer-Liszt, an unpleasant example of the showman in Liszt defeating the musician.

Liszt began the fashion of arranging Bach organ works for the piano. Compared with later arrangements by Tausig and Busoni, his versions are chaste and tasteful. He followed the originals closely and was not anxious to alter, like Tausig, who substituted vulgar octaves in both hands for the inverted mordent of the original, at the beginning of the D minor *Toccata.*

Busoni went much further than either Liszt or Tausig. His treatment was freer, sometimes the result being as much Busoni as Bach. As part of his *High School of Piano Playing* Breitkopf and Härtel published in 1900 Busoni's arrangements of ten Organ Chorale-Preludes, two Organ Preludes and Fugues, two Toccatas and the Chaconne from the fourth Violin Sonata. Of the bigger works, the C major Toccata is particularly successful. The Violin Chaconne is virtually a new piece, glorious piano writing which thunders like a cathedral organ. Brahms also made a version of this Chaconne, which does not come off so successfully, although it is far less ambitious in its scope. Other Bach unaccompanied violin pieces have also found their way on to the keyboard.

Many of Liszt's transcriptions belong to his young virtuoso days, because transcription is normally an exercise in virtuosity. Some of them, such as the *Reminiscences* of Mozart's *Don Giovanni* are nothing less than vulgar. A single piece, like the quartet from Verdi's *Rigoletto* however, is enormously successful, with its witty introduction and cascading runs over the tenor's theme.

The song arrangements are legion — Schubert, Schumann, Mendelssohn and Chopin being the most favoured. The Chopin *My Joys,* with its passionate outburst of octaves before its quiet close is Liszt at his best as an arranger. But it is in the Wagner transcriptions that the most perfect fusion occurs. Here there are no fantasias or 'pot-pourris' but realization of separate scenes from *Tristan and Isolde,* the *Mastersingers,* and the *Flying Dutchman.* Wagner was delighted with Liszt's brilliant transcription of the Overture to *Tannhäuser,* saying that when he was composing it he could hear Liszt playing it.

Liszt's *Paganini Studies* outdo the wizardry of the original violin pieces, and today remain essential studies for the pianist. *La Campanella* is a fascinating study in shimmering bell effects, with a joyous carillon chiming at the end. Busoni further 'arranged' these arrangements, the resulting effect often being artificial in merry-go-round style. Horowitz added a few flourishes of his own, so that more hyphens were added, Paganini-Liszt-Busoni-Horowitz.

Horowitz has also made a number of transcriptions and variations of his own. His two versions of *Variations on a Theme from Carmen* illustrate his different approaches to music in the 1930's and 1960's. The earlier version was spontaneous and fresh, that of the post-second World War period like five pianists playing at once; 'canned' piano-playing, but exciting nevertheless. His arrangement of the 'Stars and Stripes' is a Lisztian piece of vulgarity; that of the Mendelssohn-Liszt Wedding March even more gaudy. He has also made changes to the texts of some of the Liszt Rhapsodies, which are no improvement on the original. It is better not to 'touch up' Liszt.

The arch-arranger Leopold Godowsky, made one of the worst offences against artistic taste, when he 'arranged' the Chopin Studies to make them more difficult. He made a nauseous cocktail from the two G flat major Studies of Op. 10 and Op. 25; took the elegiac Study in E flat minor Op. 10, a wonderful essay in tone-colour between melody and accompaniment, and transformed the left hand into tasteless swirling figuration. His arrangement of Saint-Saëns' tranquil picture of *The Swan*, is a mixture of hurdy-gurdy and teashop, but it retains a sinister fascination for some pianists. This poor bird has suffered innumerable agonies since. *Le Cygne* was made into *The Dying Swan* for Anna Pavlova. Some of Godowsky's other arrangements are more acceptable and in the Albeniz *Tango* he embellishes grace-fully without vulgarity.

Towards the end of the nineteenth century a fashion, begun by Carl Tausig, for arranging Strauss waltzes as concert display pieces, reached a frenzy in the hands of Dohnanyi, Godowsky, Rosenthal, Schulz-Evler and others, who dressed up these charming waltzes in tawdry spangles. These effusive concoctions still have an appeal to unsophisti-cated audiences. They are the musical equivalent of putting on ostrich feathers to do the washing-up.

CHAPTER 4

SOME ADJUNCTS TO STYLE

Criticism

> Sympathy and knowledge, honesty and courage are the
> four qualities critics ought to possess. It is therefore very
> sad for the realm of music criticism, in many respects so
> useful, that it should often be the occupation of heads by
> no means gifted with these qualities.
>
> C.P.E. Bach Autobiography

Press criticism has a very important part to play in apprais-
ing musical performance stylistically, but whether it is
valuable or not depends on the critic's background. Generally speaking wisdom as a critic comes with maturity; it is not
advisable to let the young and inexperienced burst into
printed criticism, any more than it is prudent to allow them
to burst into performance on the concert platform.

At twenty-one I was quite confident. I knew all about
piano-playing. On first hearing Ignaz Friedman in 1940
I disliked the greater part of his recital. In 1975 I remember
details of that concert with the most appreciative retrospec-
tive pleasure. There were many things of which as a 'know-
ledgeable student' I did not approve; after thirty years
experience of listening and playing I realise it was playing of
a distinction one cannot hear nowadays.

A good critic can write a notice after a concert which is
another work of art. Yet how rarely is there an aesthetic approach to criticism. The critic often becomes a Beckmesser,
listing faults. If he is worth anything he should be equally on

his mettle to give as memorable an experience as the artist.

Too often a critic gives the impression that he is superior to both composer and performer. A. B. Walkley's criticisms of the first performances of Ibsen's plays in England were models of what criticism can be. Nobody reading them can fail to gain a deeper appreciation of Ibsen. Although a work and its performer are complementary, finally it is the creator who is more important. George Bernard Shaw's excursions into music criticism were clever and witty, as one would expect, but hardly helpful musically. It is not much use saying that the Sonata in A flat major, Op. 110 is the best of all Beethoven Sonatas; what Shaw meant was that he liked it best.

Nor is it wise to say, as some critics do nowadays, that never can such-and-such a work have received a better performance. What the critic means is that he has never heard a better performance of it (since the last time). A critic usually praises a performance if the work is played as he wants to hear it played. Often instead of being grateful for what an artist has to give, he enumerates qualities that he lacks. Although a critic can help or hinder an artist he cannot kill his career. He can only attack or wound.

Musicians usually hate critics, yet the informed critic can be the musician's best friend, and like most close friends he occasionally tells unpalatable truths. Criticism however which deteriorates into rudeness should be discounted, for after a time it can produce an atmosphere opposed to artistic effort, a philistinism which has been only too evident in English musical life over the years. In September 1959, José Iturbi after giving a Chopin recital at the Festival Hall in London was informed by the anonymous critic of *The Times* that it 'sounded as though he had not looked at Chopin's scores for years'. Only a few weeks later there were references in the same newspaper to the Chopin Study in thirds in B major and to the concluding 'rondo' of the Appassionata Sonata, errors that no first year student at a music academy would make. Those who pontificate on musical performance should themselves be above ludicrous mistakes.

It is easier to criticise than to perform. It would be very

interesting if those music critics of the London press who
are so adept at telling pianists how they should play,
composers how they should compose, conductors how they
should conduct, would get up in public and give a demonstration of their skill. They are quite ready in some cases to
advertise themselves as pianists.

One critic who can write as well as any artist plays is
Joan Chissell of *The Times*. Her notice of a harpsichord
recital by **Rafael Puyana** (*The Times* 16–3–70) at the Queen
Elizabeth Hall in London, was a welcome note in English
criticism—as refreshing and rare as rain in a desert:

Style and Imagination

> We all know what Haydn meant when urging a lady
> friend to discard her harpsichord in favour of the new
> fortepiano, 'so that everything may be better expressed'.
> Yet every now and again a harpsichordist comes along
> with a way of making it seem the most richly expressive
> instrument music has known.
>
> Rafael Puyana is one of them. His programme at the
> Queen Elizabeth Hall last night was devoted to three
> composers all living at the same time and sharing many
> of the same figures of speech. Yet from the same instru-
> ment he drew sonority unmistakably French, German
> and Italian.
>
> Watteau is the name that Mellers so frequently equa-
> tes with Couperin, and in the 15th Ordre it was easy to
> see why—most of all in Mr. Puyana's beautifully delicate
> ornamentation and transparent textures in the lullaby
> 'Dodo', the murmuring middle section of Les Vergers
> fleuris and the featherweight echoes of L' Evaporée.
> The concluding La Princesse de Chabeuil was a chat-
> terbox of uncommon grace and charm. In the two
> musettes, where Couperin flirts with the popular idiom,
> Mr. Puyana's registration brought bag-pipers on to the
> platform.
>
> For Bach's Prelude, Fugue and Allegro (BWV 998)
> and Overture in the French style Mr. Puyana changed
> from lightness and fancy to fullness and depth. But in

the bigger work the French spirit rightly prevailed in splendidly spirited tempo and buoyant rhythm. Repeats brought significant changes of registration, not least in the Sarabande where it was as if a solo statement was taken up in rich chorus. But in the concluding Echo Mr. Puyana pushed dynamic contrasts to extremes: the 'piano' echoes were barely audible.

In Bach's arrangement of Vivaldi's D major Violin Concerto Mr. Puyana entered yet another world with his flamboyant brilliance in the outer movements, and sensuous warmth in the Larghetto. His differentiation of solo and tutti was also remarkable.

—Joan Chissell, *The Times* (16–3–70).

Editions

The text from which he works is of prime importance to the conscientious pianist. There are so many bad editions of music in current use that it is a pleasure to discover the five volumes of piano pieces published by Oxford University Press with splendid introductions and notes by Howard Ferguson. Three volumes are devoted to early keyboard music, French, English, German and Italian, one to classical and one to romantic piano music. It would be very interesting if a similar volume of twentieth century piano music were now issued.

No praise can be too high for this collection; it is a commendable anthology of keyboard music from the sixteenth to the nineteenth centuries, with the sources of the texts named, and a very valuable commentary giving the historical background, descriptions of the instruments current in the period, and suggestions on ornamentation and pedalling given. There is a welcome absence of any 'doctoring' of the text. It is printed plain and unadorned.

Players do not always know which are the composer's, and which are the editor's markings. Sometimes it is a puzzle to find the composer, so cluttered up with editorial markings has the text become. Eighteenth century and earlier music has suffered dreadfully at the hands of nineteenth century editors. The Sonatas of Domenico Scarlatti have been 'touched up' by editors such as Emil Sauer. Of course some of their ideas are sensible but a player is much safer with Ralph Kirkpatrick's Edition of 60 *Sonatas* (Schirmer). The complete collection of Longo is tasteful, but he has added expression marks and sometimes altered notes.

Bach, Haydn, Mozart and Beethoven have been published in original or 'Urtext' editions, which are very valuable to the pianist concerned with style. Walter Emery in his timely *Editions and Musicians* (Novello 1951) pointed out that editors should always name the sources of their texts. Too many editions merely print the word 'Urtext' without specifying where the text came from. Von Bulow's edition of the Beethoven Sonatas is no help to stylistic performance, although his comments are interesting. His over-lavish metronome markings should be ignored, as also the proliferation of dynamic marks. Not all bad editing was done in the nineteenth century. The Associated Board edition of the Mozart Sonatas (York Bowen and Aubyn Raymar) is a classic example of over-editing.

Chopin has almost as many texts as editions. There are innumerable varying readings owing to Chopin's music being published in France, Germany and England simultaneously. His works were published first in Paris from his autograph, then in Germany from manuscript copies. He sometimes made alterations in a proof copy, which he did not note down in the autograph. At other times the pieces might be published from pupils' manuscript copies, which had suggestions added later by the composer. The French first editions are assumed to be the most authentic, but at times their readings are not as tasteful as those in other editions. Editors have often added their own conglomeration of expressive and dynamic markings. There is a mazurka in the O.U.P. Romantic period collection of Howard Ferguson which is refreshingly free from extraneous markings, and the O.U.P. has also a complete Chopin edition by Edouard Ganche. All the pianist can do is to seek the plainest text possible (the Warsaw Edition by Paderewski and others is an excellent basic text from which to work), and where there are varying readings in different edition, choose the one he thinks best. Friedman had access to the German manuscripts for his edition by Breitkopf and Härtel.

Some nineteenth century pianists were very free with texts, not hesitating to alter notes if they felt the music was badly written, or making interpolations at will. Liszt was adept at this. But today's pianist usually prefers to stick to the letter and not alter anything.

Pedalling

The pedals on the piano require as much stylistic care as the keyboard. The first principle in pedalling is discretion. The sustaining pedal can help to lessen the limitations of the instrument in maintaining the sound. Gerald Moore in *Am I too Loud?* (Hamish Hamilton, 1962) complains that a perfect legato cannot be obtained in the slow movement of the Sonata in F Minor, Op. 57 of Beethoven. The repetition of some notes certainly prevents an exact legato which might be obtained by a quartet of stringed instruments. But by delaying the depression of the pedal until the half-beat, an illusion of perfect legato can be created. Some effects can be made by the sustaining pedal which are unique to the piano. In the Chopin Scherzo in C sharp minor the last chord of the 'chorale' theme can be held while the cascading figure makes its rippling descent.

Beethoven's pedal marks have to be adjusted with care to the modern instrument, which is so much more powerful than his. Tovey in the Associated Board edition has added his own pedalling suggestions, which confuses the issue. Anton Rubinstein used to say that pedal marks in Chopin were 'all wrong'. His piano like that of Beethoven was much weaker than the later nineteenth century instrument.

Normally the sustaining pedal is best used just after a note is played, but 'circumstances alter cases'. For a special effect, as for example at the beginning of Ravel's *Jeux d'eau,* the sustaining pedal is best depressed before the opening notes are played. All kinds of subtle effect can be obtained through 'half-pedalling' i.e. releasing the pedal a little way so as not to lose all the sound. Half-pedalling is particularly helpful to get atmospheric effects, as in Debussy's *Reflets dans l'eau.* Where there is no middle pedal to sustain a long

A Steinway piano.

Peter Cooper at a Steinway piano.

The author.

bass note, half-pedalling may have to be the substitute.

Extra care must be taken in pedalling where two-piano works are played. It is better left to one of the players alone, to prevent swamping the music. The soft pedal should only be used when the hands cannot make a quieter sound. On the heavy contemporary piano however its use becomes necessarily frequent.

CHAPTER 5

STYLE IN ENSEMBLE PLAYING

It is difficult to reconcile the sound produced by a stringed instrument with that of the pianoforte. Struck chords and overtones of the piano do not match the finely-drawn sound of stretched strings set in motion by a bow. Tchaikovsky complained of the lack of blend between the two, and the piano of his day was by no means as powerful as ours.

The piano for which Schumann wrote his piano quintet was even weaker. How much more difficult it is for the contemporary pianist to play this work with the required enthusiasm and energy, yet at the same time lighten his touch to avoid swamping the quartet of strings. The tumultuous last movement of the Franck quintet is easier for him, because the organ-like breadth of the piano-writing suits the contemporary piano, and the strings are so pitched that the piano does not drown them—their heads are above water so to speak. The problem of balance is much more formidable in Franck's Violin and Piano Sonata.

Unless there is an especial acoustic reason (as in a recording), it is better for the piano lid to be kept shut in chamber music, and not partially open on the 'short stick', as the forces are too heavily weighted against the strings. This may make the dull booming of the contemporary piano even more dull, but at least it diminishes some of it.

Chamber music playing, in spite of these problems, can do nothing but good to the solo pianist, as it keeps his musical faculties at their keenest. The discipline of playing with others is excellent, the chamber repertoire of such high quality, that it demands playing of corresponding intelligence. No sloppy or careless playing will suffice here.

In a piano concerto, where the piano is the weaker protagonist, being pitted against 100 or more orchestral players, the problem of balance is quite different. In some concertos, particularly in the first movement of the Rachmaninoff second Piano Concerto, the battle is one-sided, through the heaviness of the orchestral scoring. In this concerto Rachmaninov was treating the piano more as an orchestral instrument. It is left to the conductor to secure a satisfactory balance. In concerto playing the pianist can show consideration for the orchestra at all times by maintaining a steady tempo, and he need not drown a solo instrument when the piano is merely acting in a decorative or accompanying capacity.

A concerto needs as much care in preparation as any other work on an orchestral programme, but too often a conductor seems to regard it as an unfortunate interruption to a concert. Sometimes he does not even bother to go over the work beforehand with the soloist. A concerto is more often than not under-rehearsed, the orchestral playing ragged and rough.

Mention has already been made of the appalling difficulties in presenting a Mozart piano concerto in the twentieth century. Sometimes the strings tend to sharpen in the opening tutti which is disconcerting when the soloist enters. It seems hard for the main body of strings to realize their accompanying role; there are times when they well might whisper their parts, if they are not to obscure the soloist's melodic line.

The magical hushed opening of the Beethoven fourth, surely the hardest beginning of any piano concerto, is particularly difficult to realize on the contemporary piano. It can sound metallic on our unpoetic instrument.

The concert grand may be unstylistic in a Mozart concerto; it is fatal in a concerto originally written for the harpsichord. The modern harpsichord is essential to a Bach clavier concerto, and in a small hall the string forces may be reduced to a double string quartet, plus double-bass.

One contemporary conductor, who favours the grandiloquent in all music, uses a harpsichord with electronic amplification in a baroque concerto, to match the large body of strings in a large hall.

The piano accompanist has an unenviable task on the contemporary piano. Until piano-makers return to manufacturing instruments with a lighter touch and a more sympathetic tonal quality, the problems of ensemble playing involving the piano will remain acute.

CHAPTER 6

STYLISTIC INTERPRETATION

No amount of research or theorizing will make a pianist; he must be born with a gift to communicate to others through a keyboard. How far he will succeed depends on his personality, cultural background, stamina, mental equipment, experience of life and sense of style. Superficially he may be successful by possessing a flair for brilliant playing, receiving admiration from those whose judgment is superficial. Whether he will be an artist is quite another matter. If so, he will never be satisfied, but always strive to reach a higher level. As Margot Fonteyn put it: 'At least Everest has a top—in art there is no summit.'

The Oxford Dictionary gives the meaning of interpretation as 'the rendering of a musical composition according to one's conception of the author's idea.' That conception may be quite different from the author's, but if there is one, at least there will be some resulting interpretation, not merely a presentation. Whereas a run-of-the-mill pianist leaves you in much the same state of mind, an artist gives you an experience by which you are taken out of yourself, and become identified with the work he is playing.

What makes musical performance bearable is that there is room for many different views of a work. Otherwise it would be dreadfully dull. The piano is not a machine to be set in motion like a pianola, although some pianists by their playing might make you think so. Eileen Joyce was a pianist whose playing was so mechanically perfect, that she gave the illusion that player and piano were one marvellous precision instrument. The piano is a complicated piece of mechanism which requires a human being to bring it to life, a medium through which an artistic message can be conveyed.

Although music is, in the familar cliché, an international language it would better be called national, as each country has its own stylistic musical speech. Music is organized sound, with a language of notes, or symbols, which have certain associations for us, according to our perception of them. Between East and West there is an even wider gulf than that between individual countries. Indians often consider Western music 'cold'; Westerners may be nonplussed by Eastern music. The symbols or associations connected with each are as meaningless to the other as their speech.

The most important parts of a performance are the work and its composer. It behoves the player not to put himself between the music and us. If he is in effect saying to the audience 'Listen to me, watch me,' instead of 'Listen to the work, think of the composer,' sincerity in interpretation disappears. Distressing mannerisms or unnecessary facial contortions can be external impediments to interpretation. A good actor is self-effacing, losing his personality in the character he is portraying. The good interpreter loses himself in the work he is playing.

'There are the notes, there is what is behind the notes, there is what is between the notes,' was Ignaz Friedman's dictum. A young pianist as a rule merely plays the notes. It is quite natural at his stage. Later, as he matures, more appears 'behind the notes'. It is interesting to watch the development of a pianist over the years. Sometimes there is an opposite process, and we are aware of interpretative 'devaluation' instead of development. A player at twenty plays the same work differently at forty. Where he might have been preoccupied with its notes, as a young man, now he does not worry about them. Difficulties have receded as technical mastery has increased; what seemed of long duration, now passes in a few minutes. He sees the work as a whole, as well as its parts. The score has not changed, but his conception of it has, through his experience of playing and of life. It has more intensity of meaning now, because he feels more deeply, and is not afraid to express what he feels. The young are often shy in expressing themselves.

What is between the notes is a matter of the player's personal style. Playing is not a metronomic succession of notes stabbed on to a keyboard with the relentless jab of a typewriter. Each player has a natural freedom. It is not a question of playing out of time through carelessness or bad habit, but timing a phrase in the same way as speech, so that it has a natural rise and fall, a natural spacing between the words. One big difference between today's pianists and those of fifty years ago is in their rubato. Older pianists played with more freedom.

Liszt's three requirements of technique, technique and more technique are as far as some think they need strive. Technique is an essential requirement, but it is not all. It is concerned with many other matters than mere fluency, or as Matthay said, 'scampering over the keys'. Tone production and touch are as much technical matters as speed. Technique is useful in that the music may be presented as eloquently and easefully as possible. Its aim should be that the listener is not aware of any difficulty, and can concentrate on the music itself.

The first hindrance to good interpretation can be the piano itself. If a pianist is battling with an unsympathetic, badly regulated instrument naturally it is difficult to convey any conception of a work. He may be exercised in getting an adequate performance of the notes, let alone what is behind or between them. The ideal is for him to feel that the piano is 'playing itself' not that he is having an all-in-wrestle with it, making continual adjustments in order that there may be a modicum of fluency.

The nervous system often militates against a good interpretation by causing insecurity of notes. Nervousness is a lack of confidence in front of others. It is nothing unusual; most people are naturally 'keyed up' for a performance. The better the artist, the more the strain. Taking tranquillizers or drugs is no way out. An artist has to endure it, trying not to think of himself, but of the music.

If he is playing without a score, the conventional practice, fear of a slip may induce more nervousness. Memory is largely familiarity with a work. If it is known confidently, has been performed many times in public, the player is unlikely to be very nervous about it. If a pianist wishes to use a score for a particular work, why not? There is a lot of nonsense associated with the convention of playing from memory. It is customary to use a score in chamber music. Even then accidents and nervousness occur.

Memory playing is easier in solo work, because the pianist is able to concentrate more freely on the music itself, without keeping his eyes glued on the printed notes. But it does not mean that those who use the score throughout a recital cannot give interpretatively illuminating performances. Playing from memory is also helpful to the performer in seeing the work from the outside. The workman on his own particular part of a building and the architect looking at it from the outside, have different points of view. The interpreter must be able to see part and whole at the same time. Often the best study of a work is done away from the piano, without the instrusion of fingers. Sometimes the best ideas come when away from the score altogether, when it is being gone over in the mind. Some advocate first learning a work away from the keyboard. This may be useful to a conductor because others are going to do the actual playing for him, but some time or other the pianist has to get to know where the notes lie under the hand.

It is the mind which controls interpretation. A pianist's ability to think quickly is just as important as supple fingers. He does not lose his technique because he may happen to be away from his instrument for a time. He may become physically 'rusty' but technique is as much mental as physical.

Stylistic interpretation demands of a player that he seek out the sound appropriate to a composer, and to his thought. It may mean a compromise between the contemporary instrument and that for which the work was composed. The success of an interpretation is the stylistic awareness of the player through whom the composer and the work are speaking.

At the same time piano-playing mirrors a person, his whole being. As he is, so he plays.